PORLOCK
IN THOSE DAYS
DENNIS CORNER

Porlock circa late 1950s.

PORLOCK
IN THOSE DAYS
DENNIS CORNER

EXMOOR BOOKS

© Dennis Corner

First published 1992

EXMOOR BOOKS
Dulverton, Somerset

Trade sales enquiries:

Westcountry Books
Chinon Court
Lower Moor Way
Tiverton. EX16 6SS

Tel: (0884) 243242
Fax: (0884) 243325

*Exmoor Books is a Partnership between
The Exmoor Press and Exmoor National Park*

British Library Cataloguing in Publication Data
A CIP Catalogue Record for this book is available from the British Library

ISBN 0 86183 219 1

*The publishers gratefully acknowledge the financial assistance of D.J.Miles & Co., Tea and Coffee Merchants, of Porlock,
towards the production of this book.*

Designed for Exmoor Books by
Topics Visual Information
397 Topsham Road
Exeter EX2 6HD
(0392) 876800

Typeset by Bovey Tracey TeleCottage
(0626) 835757

Front cover illustration: The old Castle Inn, late 1880s. Porlock Weir horse bus on right.

Printed in Great Britain by Sprint Print Ltd, Exeter

CONTENTS

INTRODUCTION

I was born in Somerset at Worle, then a small village outside Weston-Super-Mare, now a great sprawling place of housing estates. I lived there until, at the age of six, I moved with my mother to live with her parents at Porlock, my father having died. Porlock had been the family home of my mother's people for generations, so I think I am practically a native of the place.

My boyhood days spent with other lads of the village were wonderful days. We roamed the countryside looking at the wildlife, more plentiful and varied then. Local farmers were very tolerant, and didn't object to us walking in their fields, but we did know not to walk in crops or in a field which was let up for hay, and we didn't break down gates or hedges.

Often in our escapades, I and others fell in the rivers or the sea, or the marsh. I think for several years I had perpetual wet feet.

This and life at school, clubs, Scouts and so on, gave me a great love of Porlock, and its beautiful surroundings. Later in my working days, and in the village organisations, I met and talked with so many interesting people that I began to make notes of what they told me, and this, together with reading about the area, visiting places around and walking many miles over the moor, gave me the idea for this book.

I hope that the reader will find it interesting.

DENNIS CORNER

PORLOCK BAY

from

Katerfelto

by G. J. Whyte-Melville (1875)

High-water in Porlock Bay. The tide upon the turn. Sand-pipers, great and small, dipping, nodding, stalking to and fro, or flitting along its margin waiting for the ebb; a gull riding smoothly outside on an untroubled surface, calm as the soft sky overhead, that smiled lovingly down on the Severn Sea. Landward, a strip of green and level meadows, fringed by luxuriant woodlands, fair with the gorgeous hues of summer; stalwart oak, towering elm, spreading walnut, stately Spanish chestnut, hard mountain ash, and scattered high on the steep, above dotted thorns and spreading hazels, outposts, as it were, of delicate feathering birches, to guard the borders of the forest and the waste; fairyland brought here to upper earth, with all its changing phases, and variety of splendour.

Porlock Bay to Hurlstone Point. From above Birchanger Farm.

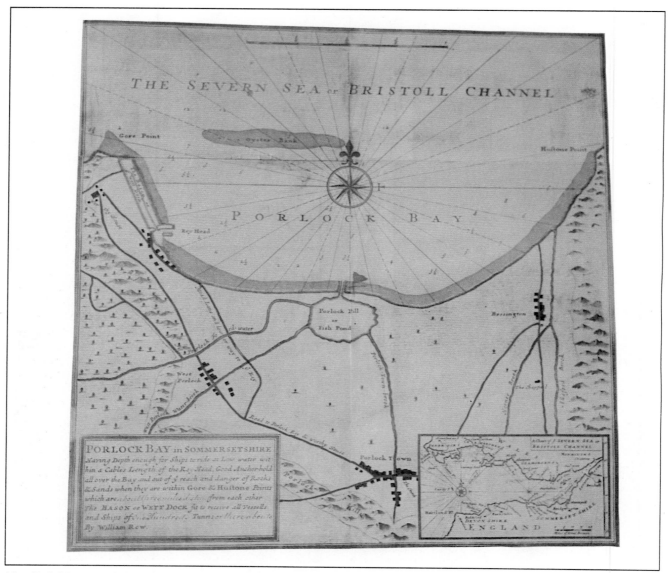

Map of Porlock Bay, prepared in the period 1710-20. Note oyster bed in the bay, and old way to Porlock Weir.

1

SOME NOTES ON PORLOCK

Porlock in West Somerset is an ancient village situated in a very sheltered valley and open to the Bristol Channel. Its name, believed to be of Saxon origin, means the locked port indicating that it always had trade by the sea. Some historians believe that there was at one time a harbour on what is now Porlock Marsh, since there is no mention of Porlock Weir, or the present harbour before the fifteenth century. It is possible too that Sparkhayes Lane, a very deep lane, which runs to the beach from near the centre of the village, had been used extensively for transporting goods up from the port. However, it might have been dug out as a boundary, many early boundaries being deep ditches with hedges a-top the banks. Again it may just have been the bed of a stream.

The earliest map of Porlock Manor dated 1710 shows Porlock Marsh as a large pill or fish pond with an outlet to the sea. Pill is a name well known along the Bristol Channel meaning a tidal creek or harbour. The outlet is shown near New Work, the name for the present outlet. This, with its sluice gate which should close on the incoming tide, was built during a big drainage scheme in about 1910, when it was hoped to drain Porlock Marsh. A previous scheme had been carried out in 1825, where already there was a decayed sluice and tunnel. Later attempts to drain the marsh have been made, notably by the Somerset River Board in the 1960s, although the Chief Engineer said at the time that they would never drain it completely because the high tides are higher than the land behind the pebble ridge, and the sea just percolates through the pebbles, or occasionally comes over the top of the beach. The pebble ridge is a remarkable natural phenomenon, which stretches from Hurlstone Point to Gore Point west of Porlock Weir, forming the semi-circle of Porlock Bay and protecting the land.

The coast must have changed at various times, and even during this last century there are regular reports of landslips at Porlockford and in the Culbone Woods. At Porlockford and Porlock Weir a sea wall was built and has had to be extended. At low water, at Redsands, opposite West Porlock there are still remains of the submarine forest, which, it is believed, was woodland thousands of years ago.

The Horner Water reaches the beach at Bossington, where it normally fills up a large pond known as the Avon Pool and the water seeps through the pebbles to the sea. On some occasions when there is a very high river after continuous heavy rain, the amount of water is so great that the pond fills up and the water floods back in a huge lake towards Bossington. The pressure builds up until eventually the water pushes the stones away, and with a mighty rush makes its outlet to the sea, forming a channel through the ridge, often 20 or so feet deep. The outlet fills up again as high tides bring in pebbles once more.

High tides coinciding with high winds have sometimes

The sea breaches the beach at Porlockford. After the storm January 25th 1990.

caused considerable flooding on the marsh. In 1859 100 sheep were drowned and in 1910 the new golf course washed away. In 1963 63 sheep were drowned, and in the spring of 1990 two large breaks were made in the pebble ridge, moving hundreds of tons of boulders and shingle, and flooding the marsh and the lower fields. This storm was the worst in the memory of many Porlock folk.

From Hurlstone Point there is a good view of the pebble ridge and the lines where the various tides have left their mark are clear to see. The beach is somewhat like the Chesil Beach at Portland. An old map of Bossington Farm names the field near Bossington Lime Kiln as 'Chesil'.

On the map of 1710 is shown a lower road to Porlock Weir which left the present road just before West Porlock and followed the Court Lease Lane (Cow Lane) to cross the stream below Porlockford and follow through beside the beach to Porlock Weir. The other road to the Weir is the present Top Road. The Lower Road as we know it was not built until the last century.

Bossington Beach from Hurlstone Point. Note tide lines on beach.

2
EARLY TIMES IN PORLOCK

Early man lived, hunted, and later farmed on Exmoor leaving various earthworks and standing stones as marks of his presence. Nearby are the Iron Age or Celtic enclosures of Bury Castle at Selworthy, Berry Castle at the top of Hawkcombe Head and Sweetworthy Camp above Cloutsham. There are also many Bronze Age burial mounds in the Dunkery area and on Culbone Hill. The best known is Alderman's Barrow. A stone row, and a stone with a wheeled cross on it believed to be sixth century, can also be seen on Culbone Hill. There is a stone circle at Colly Water.

The Whitstones on Porlock Hill.

Most prominent of the standing stones are the Whitstones which lie between the junction of the A39 and the Exford Road. Legend has it that these stones were thrown in contest from Hurlstone Point by the Devil and St Peter (or even St Dubricius).

Other traces of ancient man have been found: I have seen worked arrow heads discovered in a field above Selworthy as well as chippings of flint from Hawkcombe Head. In Taunton museum are the oldest human remains found on Exmoor. This skeleton was unearthed in 1896 by a man digging stones for road repairs in the quarry on the A39 beyond the entrance to Broom Street Farm. The man had been buried in a cyst or kistvaen, a form of coffin made of stone slabs. With him was buried a pot or beaker with a decorated edge. Archaeologists have dated the tomb to c.1500 BC.

The Celts who inhabited Bury Castle and Sweetworthy left traces of their language in a few local place-names such as Myne on North Hill and Dunkery itself. The Roman invasion made little impression in this area although there were fine Roman cities as near as Bath and Exeter. All we have is Old Burrow, the still visible Roman fort above Glenthorne, once garrisoned by 80 soldiers under a centurion. Soon deserted for another fort at Martinhoe, this lookout had a fine view of the channel and across to Wales where the Silures still resisted Roman domination. Maybe the names Broomstreet, Brandish Street and Stratford were derived from a road or street once leading to the fort.

Around about 700 AD the Saxons began to invade and settle in the area. Many place names such as Selworthy, Bossington, Luccombe and Porlock itself date from this time as the valley was cleared for farms. That the area was thinly populated is confirmed by the Domesday Survey taken twenty years after the Norman Conquest in 1066. At the time there were six villeins, three bordars and six slaves recorded in Porlock. If these represented heads of families it would be unlikely that there were more than about 100 people living there.

On two occasions earlier Porlock had been the scene of Viking invasions. The second attack in 1052 involved Harold, son of Godwin, later to be King of England for a brief time. He and his brother raised a small army, and with nine ships sailed into Porlock Bay. They landed at a spot between Porlock and Porlock Weir – there is a field which goes by the name of 'Hellbyes' near Porlockford where, during the last century, fragments of weapons were found. Numbers flocked to resist the invasion, but Harold and his well drilled body of men, with nothing before them but to do or die, succeeded in reaching Porlock, burnt every building and carried off what spoil they could. Thirty thanes and great numbers of other people were slain that day.

Collinson, in his *History of Somerset* (1750) said that the men of Porlock used to point out remains of buildings which had been burnt, as they supposed, at the great foray of Harold. The utter destruction of Porlock at that time would indicate that no part of the church is dated earlier than 1051, although a piece of Saxon cross was found at a much later date, and can be seen there. It is believed to be the oldest worked stone in any church in the district.

From the Domesday Book we learn that the Lord of the Manor of Porlock before the Conquest was Algar, who is identified as the son of Leofric, Earl of Mercia.

On the coming of the Conqueror the lands were conferred upon Baldwin, Bishop of Exeter, as overlord. The Domesday description of Porlock reads: 'Baldwin has a Manor called Portloc, which Algar held before 1066 and rendered geld for three hides. Twelve teams can plough it. Roger, son of Nigel holds it of Baldwin, and has one hide and a half in demesne and the villeins have the other lands. Rogo has there six villeins, three bordars, six serfs, 300 acres of wood and 500 acres of pasture. It is worth 25 shillings, when Baldwin received it, it was worth 4 pounds'.

There seems little reason to doubt that Rogo was of the Roges family which held the manor down to the time of Edward III. Many of the Roges bore the name Simon. There used to be a meadow in Villes Lane where it joined Furzeland Road called 'Simon's Meade', now built on; a name attributed to one of the Roges.

Later the manor was held by Sir Nigel Loring, who, in the year 1366, was granted a market to be held on Thursday of every week; also three fairs annually within the manor, each fair lasting three days. By the same charter, Sir Nigel had leave to impark his woods at Porlock and preserve the game. To the present day the woods to the west of Porlock are known as 'The Parks'. There is a deep ditch and bank which marks the boundary at the top of higher 'Park' above the Toll Road, probably dug at the time the Park was made.

Visiting Porlock today we enter the High Street from the Minehead direction down the old steep or original way, known as Dunster Steep, which leads to the part of Porlock known as Dovery or Doverhay. The Steep belonged, prior to 1930, to the Parish of Luccombe. The Dovery part of Luccombe stretched as far as the beach in a long arm known as the Luccombe corridor, which gave Luccombe its own access to the sea.

Dovery is mentioned as a separate manor in the Domesday Book where it states: 'Roger has a Manor called Doveri which Edema held before 1066 (in the reign of Edward) and rendered geld for one virgate. One team can plough it. Alric holds it of Roger, Alric has there two villeins and one bordar, and it is worth 7 shillings and 6 pence. When Roger received it, it was worth 10 shillings'.

Porlock was divided from its small neighbour Dovery by a stream which today runs from the main Hawkcombe Stream to the Recreation Ground, through the Rectory land and under the Drang into 'Tinker's Orchard'. Passing between Rawles Buildings and Lowerbourne it runs under the main street near the newsagents and finally back into the Hawkcombe Stream again. The old boundary was the main street from the newsagents to where another stream passes under the road near the entrance to England's Road.

This meant that people living in Lowerbourne, or Bond's and Marley's Rows belonged to the Parish of Luccombe, as can be witnessed by the names of some of the Dovery people on the War Memorial Roll of Honour in Luccombe Church. As children they would have been taken to church at Luccombe where their allegiance was. In fact, as late as 1928, a petition was organised by residents of Dovery asking that they remain in the Parish of Luccombe, as there was a proposal to bring Dovery into Porlock.

3
THE CHURCH
OF ST DUBRICIUS

Porlock parish church is dedicated to St Dubricius or St Deveroe as he used to be called. The Welsh knew him as Dyfrig. He is believed to be have been born about 450 AD in Madley six miles west of Hereford. A lot is known about his activities in Herefordshire from a record of land grants made to him by the reigning kings in order to found Llans (churches). As a bishop he was wise, and a great teacher. He is co-patron of Llandaff Cathedral and patron of several churches in Herefordshire. There is a chapel dedicated to him in Llandaff. It is mainly due to Dubricius that Hereford embraced and fostered the Christian faith a century before St Augustine came to Canterbury in 597 AD. Dubricius is said to have crowned King Arthur, and married him to Queen Guinevere. He lived to a great age spending his later years as a hermit on Bardsey Island. He died c.546 AD. A stained glass window in the tower in memory of the Rev. Walter Hook, depicts St Dubricius. Whether he ever visited Porlock is not known, but what may be regarded as certain is that the first church in Porlock was founded by St Dubricius or someone in close association with him.

The cross-legged effigy in the arched recess in the south aisle is of a knight in chain armour of the thirteenth century. Traditionally it represents a member of the Roges, or, as they were known, the Fitz Roges family. It is believed the Fitz Roges were the builders of the present church.

About the middle of the fourteenth century the manor passed to Sir Nigel Loring, a distinguished soldier and devout churchman. At his death his estates were divided between his two daughters. Porlock fell to Isabella who married Sir Robert Harrington of Aldingham, Lancashire. She died in 1400, and he in 1406. Their son, Sir John, the 4th Baron, married Elizabeth, daughter of Edward Courtenay, 3rd Earl of Devon. Sir John went off to the French wars in 1417/18, a close supporter of King Henry V. With him went a company of 86 archers, and 29 lancers, men recruited from the Porlock district. Sir John failed to return. We do not know how he died, but he left a long will of all his bequests which included the setting up of a 'Chantry'. Two priests were to be employed to help with the work and services of the church. They were to celebrate divine service and pray for the souls of Lord and Lady Harrington's parents and ancestors. It is believed that Chantry Cottage (formerly two cottages) and probably the oldest dwelling in Porlock was where they lived.

Although Sir John Harrington died in 1417, the chantry was not set up for another 50 years. By then Lady Elizabeth had re-married to Sir William Bonville of Chewton Mendip, who was beheaded by the Lancastrians after the battle of St Albans in 1461. Lady Elizabeth spent much of her time at her manors of Porlock and Brendon until her death in 1471.

St Dubricius Church.

Houses around the church, c. 1885.

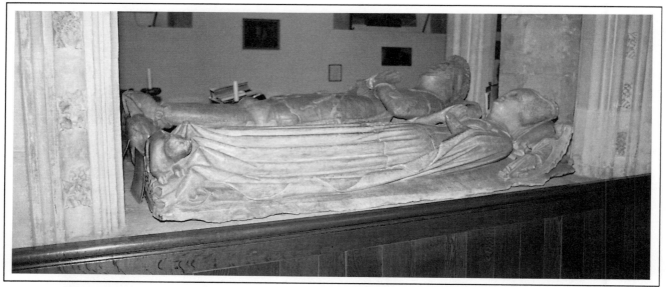

The Harrington Monument.

The monument to her and her first husband is the finest carving in the church, and said to be the finest of its kind in England. The knight wears plate armour of the period, and the lady, a beautiful dress and head-dress. The monument and canopy were once richly coloured, but the natural dyes have nearly completely faded away. The effigies are of alabaster, believed to have come from Chellaston, near Derby.

After the death of Lady Harrington, the estate passed to the Grey family, via Cecily Bonville who was Baroness Bonville and Harrington in her own right, and one of the richest women in England. At sixteen years of age she married Sir Thomas Grey, first Marquis of Dorset. The estate stayed in this family until the beheading in 1553 of Lady Jane Grey, the Nine Days' Queen.

There is an ancient clock in the church near the tower. It is one of the oldest in England and was taken down from the tower at the Diamond Jubilee of Queen Victoria, when the present clock was installed. It had neither face nor hands but merely struck the hour on the tenor bell. As everything was so much quieter, and the pace of life slower, men working in the fields or workshops would have heard the bell strike the hour. The clock is believed to date from the 1400s. In the bailiff's accounts of the Manor of Brendon, is the entry: 'for the expenses of the Bailiff in riding from Brendon to Barnstaple and returning to Porlock for Roger the Clockmaker to fetch him to the Lady: 3d.'.

In the church porch is a board commemorating Henry Rogers of Cannington. The Rogers family (not to be confused with the Roges) were Lords of the Manors of Cannington, Burnham, and Porlock in the seventeenth century. It was this Henry Rogers who gave Porlock two of its charities, namely the Rogers Charity, and the Winsford Land Charity, both of which are still in existence.

The most notable feature of Porlock church from the outside is its truncated spire, or steeple. The top is said to have been blown off in a gale about 1700. Perhaps this was the great gale of 1703, which did great damage in Somerset,

Wales and Monmouthshire. It is said that when the men were rebuilding the steeple, the stag hounds passed through the village, and being keen on hunting, they downed tools and followed the hunt, and didn't come back to finish the job! Another suggestion was that a light could be put on the top of the steeple to guide the fishermen, often fishing well into the night, when herring fishing was so important. Whatever the reason we do know that any church can have a pointed spire, but Porlock's being as it is, is unique!

Amongst the many tombstones with names of families who have lived for generations in Porlock, is one by the west corner of the tower. It is a pathetic epitaph on Thomas and Prudence Rawle, who died within a day of each other:

'He first departed; she for one
day tried to live without
Him, liked it not and dy'd.'

Up until the Second World War, the death bell or Passing Bell was rung on the death of a parishioner (for a fee). During the war the bells were silenced and would only be used in the event of invasion, or air raid. Another old custom was to rope the bride and groom at a wedding. Village children would hold a rope with a horse shoe in the middle, across the path by the church gate. The groom was expected to pay for himself and his bride to pass the gate.

A full-scale restoration was carried out during the nineteenth century while the Rev. Walter Hook was Rector. The spire was restored in 1884, and the oak shingles replaced. The church was closed in 1890 and services held in the schoolroom until another room had been fitted out and licenced. On May 28th 1891 the church was reopened by the Lord Bishop of the Diocese. All the money for the restoration was raised locally, and the work carried out by Messrs Cooksley and Huish. The parish was justly proud of the work carried out by local men. The steeple was re-shingled again in 1933. The shingles are flat pieces of Sussex oak, 9 inches x 4 inches, used like slates and fixed by copper nails.

Most of the Rectory was built in the early 18th century, but there is evidence that some parts are as early as 14th century. For many years the Rectors held what was known as the Rectory Manor. Part of their living came from the rents of cottages and gardens on this land. It was mainly in Hawkcombe, including the Mill, up as far as 'Peep Out' Cottage, where the boundary turned up to Porlock Hill, thence down the road to a point near the Ship Inn, and then back to the Rectory.

In the woods in Hawkcombe there are still small walled-in plots, which were once gardens and small-holdings, now overgrown. Some of these were used until well after the Second World War, even poultry and pigs being kept there. The land in Hawkcombe, originally used as allotments by men who sang in the church choir, is still known as the Alleluia Field. And the hill near the television mast is still known as Parsons Hill.

4

LIME KILNS AND TANYARD

There were once many lime kilns in the area, both on farms and along the coast. The most prominent one locally is on Bossington Beach. Another, now built over, is at Porlock Weir, where the fireplaces can still be seen. A third is at the bottom of Worthy Water, where it joins the beach.

Where land was too acid, lime, which is very alkaline was added by the farmers to improve the soil. At one time a substance known as marl was used; this is a type of rock that consists of almost equal amounts of calcium carbonate and clay. There were marl pits at Middlecombe, near Minehead, and at Blackford Farm, west of Brakeley Steps, near the Porlock road.

Later lime was used. There were some outcrops locally: at Newlands, near Exford, and at Alcombe, but as these were few, lime was imported to West Somerset and North Devon from South Wales, particularly from Aberthaw, near Barry. It was brought over in sailing ketches in the form of limestone as it was quarried. On the list of harbour dues at Porlock Weir on March 5th 1723 'for every ton of limestone 1d.' Where the boat was near a harbour, the boat would come in and offload, but where there was no harbour, as at Bossington, the boat would come in as near to the shore as was safe, and the cargo would be thrown overboard at high tide. As the tide ebbed a horse and cart, or donkeys with panniers or crucks were used to bring the stones to the kiln.

The kiln consisted of a strong stone building surrounding a huge pit, about 16 feet deep and about 8 feet in diameter; underneath were sometimes two or three archways. It was from these archways that the lime, when molten, dropped from a type of flue. The firing took several days; the method was to burn the limestone with culm (pronounced cullum locally), an anthracite dust, also imported from Wales.

The fire was lit with brushwood at the bottom of the flue to get the culm started; then the alternate layers of broken limestone and culm, which had been fed down the pit, would burn until red hot. After several days, when the firing was complete and the lime cool enough, it would be raked out at the bottom of the kiln, and taken away, again by donkeys from the more inaccessible places, or by pack ponies or horse and cart from others.

The lime was also used in the building trade for lime mortar, and for lime wash on both interior and exterior walls. Lime mortar was made by adding about three times its volume of sand and mixing it with water.

Lime spreading was very hard work, and both men and horses often suffered burns. The lime was taken to the fields in horse drawn butts and dropped in heaps, which were then spread by hand. Lime has been used to sweeten acid soil for over 1000 years. Slaked lime was extensively used on Exmoor by the Knight tenants when they first cleared the

Lime kiln at Bossington.

land. Exmoor, with its peat bogs, is notoriously acid, and it was found that it required about one ton of lime per acre. A track above Porlock Weir leading to Exford and the moors is still known as Lime Way.

Lime burning certainly continued into the nineteenth century. An old Exford man told me he had hauled it from Porlock Weir to Exford, then spread it on the fields. The exact date that lime burning ceased at Bossington is unknown, but there was a lime burner recorded there in the 1851 census. I suspect the burning carried on until much later. At Bossington today you can find pieces of lime and small pieces of culm scattered around the old kiln, and all the old stone walls there are held together with lime mortar.

In the 1920s and '30s more use was made of sulphate of ammonia, basic slag and superphosphates, all sold in bags, thus easing the farmer's work, and putting the lime burner out of business.

Tanning has provided employment in the area for several hundred years. Mention is made of tanners, and also the appointment of inspectors of leather in the records of the Court Leet as early as the reign of James I.

In later days the Tannery was owned by Mr Pearce, and after him, his son. The town mill, next to the Castle Inn, was rebuilt in 1898 to produce electricity for the Tannery.

To obtain the tan from the bark of the indigenous sessile oak tree, men would cut the trees in the springtime and then, with an iron tool known as a bark stripper remove the bark from the wood. The remaining wood was used for firewood and fencing posts, and the tree stumps were left to re-sprout and grow for future use. These oak woods were known as scrub oak and people would buy a 'rap of wood' for this purpose.

After ripping off the bark, and drying it, the bark would be taken to the Tannery where, near the entrance was a weigh

Stripping bark.

Barkshed at the Tannery.

Workers going to the Tanyard, c.1910-14.

bridge and office. It was stored in large sheds until wanted, and was then ground up on a machine driven by a large water wheel from the mill leat.

The hides were first soaked in a lime pit for about two weeks, to loosen the hair sufficiently for unhairing, using scrapers. The hair was sold to the building trade for mixing with plaster. Afterwards the hides were thoroughly washed and then the fleshers would remove all the fat and flesh by scraping with two-handled fleshing knives. The ground-up oak bark was soaked in pits; then the hides were saturated in this liquid, and continually moved into fresh solutions for about 12 months. They would then be hung to drip before being rolled. The tannin (tannic acid) from the oak bark seeps very slowly through the pores of the hide and drives out water, coating the fibres with preservatives. There was always a burning heap of used bark in a field below the village which gave off an obnoxious smell, as did the hides.

The pits were situated in what is now the garden of the hardware shop, the house butting on to the street being the house of Mr Pearce, the Tannery owner. Altogether about 30 men were employed. The hours were long; from six in the morning until six at night. A bell summoned the men to work and to finish. There was an early finish at 4pm on Saturdays, and no work on Sundays.

Whenever anyone living in the High Street was ill, a thick layer of tan from the Tannery would be spread in the road outside the house to deaden the sound of the horses and wagon wheels. Apparently people were very considerate about noise disturbance, more so perhaps than nowadays.

The leather was of top quality, used for harness and hunting equipment with a small quantity of best leather for footwear.

On one occasion when the firm had its outing to London; some of the men paid a visit to a pub for refreshment, and in the course of conversation with a barmaid one asked if she was busy. 'Not particularly', she replied. 'I think you will be today', she was told, 'there's thirty of us up from Porlock'.

The Tannery was closed in the early 1930s. During the Second World War it was taken over as a barracks. The 58th Company of Royal Engineers, many of whom had returned from the Dunkirk evacuation, arrived in 1941, and stayed until sent off to India in 1942. Later the American Army used the barracks, and huts for extra accommodation were built in the field behind the Tannery. These were demolished in 1945, immediately after hostilities ceased in Europe.

The buildings were subsequently used by the Exmoor Engineering Company until that business closed. The site is now divided into different units as a craft centre.

5
SMUGGLING

For hundreds of years smuggling has been carried on around the coast of Britain and particularly in the South of England because it was nearer to the coast of France. Places along the whole length of the Bristol Channel have their own tales of smuggling. In some places it was a highly organised crime, conducted by desperate men in armed luggers using bribery and threats of violence. Lynmouth, Watermouth, Ilfracombe and Lundy Island were notorious, while Heddon's Mouth was a favourite landing place, where a smuggling lugger once sailed too close to the shore and was lost with all hands. At Trentishoe no less than 262 tubs were once found under a stable floor. Minehead and Watchet together with Porlock Weir had their own resident Excise Officers, who sometimes changed sides and did a bit of smuggling themselves.

An enquiry made by the Court of Exchequer in 1559 regarding customs dues along the Somerset coast, listed seven ports and describes Porlock Bay: 'Where may ride forty or fifty ships, but there is no Quay nor safe Lying'. In 1723 Mr William Culliford, Surveyor General of H.M. Customs, visiting Porlock reported: 'I went to visit Porlock which is about four miles from Mynehead where there is a very deep Bay and a good harbour for small vessels, to which place there are several that belong, which trade over sea. The officer Richard Davis, is an active young fellow, hath hitherto been paid £5 per ann. by incident; he well deserves £10 per ann. and be stablished, it being a place of trade and where great quantities of herrings are taken and cured, which begets a great concourse of people and small craft, that may be of dangerous consequence to the Customs, unless well guarded'.

We can be certain that smuggling was carried out at Porlock since temporary hiding places abounded. There was one under the floor at Bromham Farm. While relaying the floor during the last century, a Mr Huish of Parson Street, was taken into the secret and undertook to do the work in one day. In return he was treated as a favoured customer, was well entertained and on going home fell into the water. He suffered from gout ever after. In Higher Doverhay Farm there was another such place, contrived between an inner and outer wall. A second wall had been built outside the main wall of the house at the dairy end and the thatched roof brought down to cover the space between the two. The entrance was hidden by placing a milk pan before it. When discovered at about the turn of the century the stands for the spirit kegs were still in place. Miss Clara Ridler, who lived at Doverhay Farm, told me that the little window in the chimney by the front door of the farm, was used as a look-out to Porlock Weir. A signal was passed from Doverhay Farm to the boats in the bay if the coast was clear. Nowadays Porlock Weir cannot be seen from this window since new houses block the view.

Doverhay Farm.

Another hiding place was found in about 1850 when a hunted hare disappeared below ground near Pools Wood and Bossington Lane.

A hole was dug out disclosing a chamber of 9 or 10 feet square, and over the height of a man. I was very interested when a friend who lived in Old Lane told me that he knew where this hiding place was! The Electricity Company wanted to put a stay just inside his garden, to support a post outside. They brought the digger and, when work started, the ground collapsed and the digger dropped down into a hole which he described as being a 'little room lined with bricks'. Whether this was the same hole as the one previously described, I don't know, but it is in the same area. It has now been filled in. There are many tales of encounters with Customs men. When they came searching at Chapel Knap, the old lady there sat on top of a keg, and said: 'Come inside me dears, you be welcome to search here'. They searched and found nothing, but of course the old lady's long skirt was draped over the keg. Rebecca Pollard of Porlock Weir hid a cask in her garden and covered it with a skep of bees knowing that if they came the Customs men wouldn't be likely to disturb them.

It was reported that in 1886 great casks of rum together with thousands of coconuts came ashore following the wrecking, off the Nash, of the vessel 'Mabel'. The Customs officers made their grab, but they missed a lot, for men of the Weir had already tapped some of the casks and filled smaller kegs from them, hiding them in Culbone Woods.

I remember when up to a dozen very large barrels of wine were washed ashore, and were picked up and taken to a lock-up at Pollard's Garage. The Customs and Excise men came and put their seal on the barrels. However, sad to say, the sea water had got into what, in any case, was cheap wine, so the whole lot was just drained out into the paddock. I suspect that 'in those days' the barrels would have been taken ashore without the Customs officers even knowing of them.

6
TALES MY GRANDPARENTS TOLD ME

As a small boy I remember my grandfather telling me he could remember Porlock market days. There were three annual fairs in May, August and October and also a weekly market. He said the sheep and bullocks were penned all along the street, near the Castle Inn. At one time there were as many as 1500 sheep and 200 bullocks. The hurdles were stored, when not in use, in a building where the Central Garage now is. In the last century people spoke of a Market House similar to that at Dunster, and a Market Cross. It is probable that the arrival of the railway at Minehead put a stop to Porlock Market.

Grandfather went to school in Parson Street, the fee being 3d. per day. The present school was opened in 1879. The first schoolmaster was Mr John Orchard who lived in Doverhay. Many families stayed in areas for generations, and Porlock was no exception, there being a John Orchard recorded as living in Doverhay in the 1300s in the 21st year of Henry III's reign.

As a boy grandfather was employed, as many boys were all over England in Queen Victoria's reign, in bird scaring. The corn was either sown broadcast by hand, or with a fiddle; corn drills were not used then, at least not on very steep hillsides. After the corn was sown, he would stay on Parsons Hill scaring away crows and rooks for a penny a day. The boys used either a rattle similar to that used by football supporters or a clapper which consisted of two flat pieces of wood joined by a piece of leather. With a quick flick of the wrist the two pieces would slap together and make a loud report like a gun. The boys would shout and wave their arms about too. Grandfather always used a clapper.

Grandmother's uncle, George Jarman, was a carrier for Lynch Flour Mills. Some of his deliveries with his wagon and two horses took him over Porlock Hill to Lynmouth. Once he was attacked by robbers on his way home, and had to use his whip on them. After that occasion, when he was paid for the flour, he used to hide the money in the corner of a flour bag, and put it on the wagon with all the other bags on top of it.

Grandfather used to tell me that the lord and lady whose statue is in the church were killed by a wild boar, which came out of Pools Wood near Bossington Lane. This story was used sometimes to frighten young children who misbehaved. In all probability the story arose because the lady has her feet resting on a boar, the badge of the Courtenay family.

Grandmother's family lived at Bossington, and in the days when smuggling was rife, sometimes heard the sound of horses and carts coming up from the beach at night. The curtains would be tightly drawn so that, if questioned, a truthful answer could be given that nothing had been seen. Both my grandparents' families were staunch Wesleyans, services being held in the front room of their home at Bossington before the chapel was built. John Wesley

Mr Jarman with the flour wagon from Lynch Mills, c.1880.

himself preached strongly against the smuggling trade, and didn't Rudyard Kipling in his smuggling song write

'Them that asks no questions, isn't told a lie,

Watch the wall, my darling, while the gentlemen go by'?

My great grandparents, John and Sarah Burgess lived at the lower of the two Ship Cottages, at the bottom of Redway, just above the Ship Inn. One day a man travelling with a performing bear came and asked for board and lodging for the night, which they agreed to provide. 'What shall I do with the bear?' said the man. 'Put him in the empty sty', he was told. There were two stys at the top of the garden, one for each cottage but only one in use. During the night the bear broke through the wall, killed and ate the pig in the neighbouring sty.

My grandfather often related the story of how the men at Lynmouth brought the lifeboat 'Louisa' over the hills and down to launch at Porlock Weir, during a winter night in 1889, when the schooner 'Forrest Hall' of Liverpool was in distress in Porlock Bay. He was out early with his bread deliveries when the boat arrived. There had been a last minute delay when the boat on its carriage reached the two cottages at the foot of Porlock Hill on what is still, I expect, the narrowest part of the whole of the A39, and it was even narrower in those days. It was found that they couldn't get through, so the men began to knock off the corner of the top cottage wall. The story goes that the old lady who lived in the cottage looked out the window, and shouted, 'What be you about down there?'. On being told of the ship in distress, and that they would only take a little bit off her wall and promised to come back later to repair it, she decided to get up, and as she had never seen a lifeboat before she followed on to Porlock Weir. The story of this epic launch was related for years by the older folk of the village, being probably the greatest event in their lives.

It was after this that a lifeboat station was built at Minehead in 1901, thus lessening the gap between stations.

Grandfather often spoke of another event: the great snow of 1891 when Amos Cann lost his life. The Canns lived at Greenlands Farm, near Exford, and Amos had walked to Porlock on business. It was snowing hard in the evening when he left to walk home. Local people begged him to stay the night, but he insisted on returning as he was needed to tend the sheep. He didn't arrive home; search parties and the staghounds were used to try to find him, but it was 17 days later that his body was found under a hedge, near Alderman's Barrow about a mile from home. It was thought he fell into a snow drift, and was too exhausted to get out. There is a headstone to his grave just inside the churchyard at Exford. (I once met his brother Sam, who came to live in Porlock when he was an old man. He was nearly 90 when I spoke to him).

People often had to travel long distances to work, but had no transport. Two of my grandfather's brothers were builders at Porlock. At one time they were building some houses at Barbrook Mill, above Lynmouth. They would work each week from Monday to Saturday midday, staying in lodgings. On Saturday afternoon they walked the 14 or 15 miles to their homes, spent the evening and all of Sunday with their wives, and early on Monday walked to Barbrook to work again. The Pollard Brothers of Porlock Weir also walked to and from Lynmouth for boat building work. One man walked daily from Selworthy to Exford and back, and more recently I well remember an old man walking from Selworthy to Porlock for gardening work, when he was well over 70 years old. Life was tough in those days. It was also hard for young people. Grandfather's oldest brother, William, started work at the age of 11, at Wydon Farm, near Minehead. Grandfather could remember seeing a local chimney sweep climb up inside, and sweep the larger chimneys. When he reached the top, he would look out and shout, 'Sweep all up'.

Grandfather was one of the village bakers, and used to bake and deliver bread around the village. He told me that in his early days he went to Bristol for the first time to learn the trade and he asked: 'How shall I know the way?'. The answer was: 'You've got a civil tongue in your head, haven't you?!' He bought his flour at Lynch Flour Mills, which

The Brothers Pollard – Noah and William. Caulking the seams of a vessel at Porlock Weir.

closed about 1890. The bread was risen with the aid of barm from the Sparkhayes Malt House. A portion of dough was kept each day in order to be put into the new ferment to help it to rise. It was made in the evening and left until about 3am when work would start. During the First World War they said they ate black bread, (not really black, but very dark) and in order to save flour they added a proportion of boiled potatoes to the mixture.

Grandfather told me of the big snowfall of his young days, when he had to walk to Bossington with the bread in a basket, along the tops of the hedges as the lane was full of snow. There were no houses in Bossington Lane, and no one to clear the way. Another baker, who had a bakehouse in Parson Street, was Mr Brewer, and he used to deliver bread to Porlock Weir, walking all the way with a basket on each arm.

7
METHODISM IN PORLOCK

George Whitfield was the first Methodist preacher to visit Somerset, when in 1739 he preached at Keynsham and Publow. John Wesley preached at Bath on April 10th, 1739. Wesley's prime concern was to bring his message to the working people. It is for this reason that Methodism was at its strongest in Somerset in the mining villages and cloth making towns of the county, mostly in the Mendips.

At first Wesley's preaching was opposed by the mob, often encouraged by Anglican clergymen. However, undaunted, he continued, and visited Somerset every autumn until 1790, the year before his death. Sometimes the preaching of Wesley and his followers fell on deaf ears. At Wincanton he thought the people had just as much feeling as the benches they sat on.

Wesley and his preachers continued, and it is estimated that Wesley preached 540 sermons in at least 40 towns and villages in Somerset in 51 years. The only place in Somerset west of Bridgwater that he visited was Minehead, on two occasions.

By 1790 the Methodists were established in Taunton, and Mr Giles – a tanner – from Holnicote persuaded the Taunton preacher to include this part of West Somerset in his pastorate and regular meetings were begun at Williton, Carhampton and Holnicote. In Porlock the earliest preachers came and preached in the main street and in Sparkhayes Lane either standing on a mounting block or on a chair.

By 1811 the new Dunster Circuit had been formed and this included Porlock where services were held in local homes. In 1826 there was a membership of six, plus adherents, meeting in a room in Mr Nicholas Snow's cottage, opposite the present methodist church. The Porlock Methodist Society grew until in 1836, with a membership of 30, it was decided to build a chapel. There was already a strong sunday school which had started in 1826, and in 1851 had grown to 56 members. There was also a day school.

A site was leased from the Earl of Lovelace at £1 per annum for a term of 60 years. A chapel to seat 170 was completed in 1837 at a cost of £225. The freehold was obtained in 1885, when the Earl sold Sparkhayes and other properties. The building is now the 'Countryman Cafe'. The first steward was George Rawle, master tanner, the son-in-law of Nicholas Snow. The memorials to George Rawle and his wife Mary are on the wall at the back of the present church.

By 1908 the Porlock Methodists, or Wesleyans as they were more commonly called, had decided to build a new church and acquired a piece of land opposite the Post Office. But fund raising was slow, and there was a constant migration of Methodist families to Minehead and further away. The First World War came and there was no possibility of building until, in the 1920s, a new spirit came to the

Old chapel, after Sunday morning service, c.1905.

members, and they began to raise money by subscription and special efforts. The last service in the old chapel was in March 1927 and then for three months services were held in the village hall. The new church was designed by Mr Tamlyn, a Minehead architect, and was built by Brown Bros of Porlock – a Methodist family – at a cost of £4,600.

The church is built of red sandstone from West Luccombe Quarry, a gift of the Acland family of Holnicote, and the building is faced with stone from Ham Hill, near Montacute. It was opened in June 1927 and the first sermon was preached by Rev. Dr Ferrier Hulme, the then President of the Methodist Conference. Afterwards tea was served in the village hall to nearly 500 people in three relays. After tea there was a great evening meeting presided over by Mr William Stoate of Williton, another great name in Methodism. The church, with seating for 350, was packed and chairs had to be put in the aisles – over 400 attended – and more than £970 was raised in this one evening.

There are extensive rooms below the church, and a schoolroom at the rear of the building. The premises have been well used over the years, both by the church and various other village organisations.

In 1936 a new Hammond electronic organ was purchased to replace the old hand pumped instrument and in 1970 this

FOUNDATION STONE LAYING
WESLEYAN CHAPEL, PORLOCK.

Laying the foundation stone for the new chapel, 1926.

was replaced by a pipe organ from the redundant Sunnyside Methodist Church, Weston-Super-Mare. The organ, built in 1888 by Walker of London, was rebuilt at Porlock by Messrs George Osmond, Organ Builders of Taunton. The church was filled for the opening recital given by Dudley Savage, the popular radio organist. This organ is of the traditional tracker action with the addition of a balanced swell pedal; it has two manuals and a full pedal board.

In 1981 the worship area was altered by the removal of several rows of pews, the wood being used to make a movable screen. The back area now makes a useful lounge.

Many people and their families have served the church well, and many of the sunday school scholars have gone out into the wider world, and helped to spread the gospel in their work. Some have gone as preachers, and even as missionaries and doctors to places as far afield as India.

Many local preachers were men and women from Porlock. They would often travel by horse, or pony trap in all weathers to take services in small chapels in the circuit, usually taking two or even three services on a Sunday; this after working all week. Later on, both local preachers and ministers often travelled by bicycle, bus or car, depending on the generosity of the local people for their food during their visit.

The Methodist church on the occasion of the Royal Wedding, 1981.

Porlock Methodist church is now one of sixteen which, since 1969, form the West Somerset Circuit, an amalgamation of the former Kingsbrompton, Minehead and Dunster, and Williton Circuits.

8

A SALE, A FIRE, AND A COURT CASE

On Saturday September 17th 1887 at two o'clock at the Ship Inn, there was held a large auction sale of building sites and property in Porlock and Luccombe (Luccombe meaning Dovery). This was the property of Mr Blathwayt the owner of Porlock Manor Estate. Rentals were very low and I believe the sale was a way to raise money for the improvements then needed for Porlock Weir harbour and for building the lock gates.

Lot 1 was 'the two cottages, with garden, piggery etc., situated on the Porlock and Lynton road above the Ship Inn, as now occupied by John Burgess and John Moore', at the rent of £3.10s. each per annum. (John and Sarah Burgess were my great grandparents).

Lot 14 was in the parish of Luccombe, and described as the 'Valuable premises known as 'Lurborn Court' comprising two four-roomed cottages, barn, two-stall stable, three-stall stable and cattle shed with yards, good garden and orchard. Held, with other premises by Mr R. Ridler, at the apportioned rent of £10. Note – on the Porlock side of this lot runs the public water course known as Lurborn or the Lowerbourne Water. The owner has the right to use the water for drinking purposes, and it is regarded as a public offence to pollute or divert same'.

This stream, of course, is the old boundary stream already described as the division between Dovery and Porlock.

In 1900 a disastrous fire destroyed much of this part of Dovery. It started on Shrove Tuesday in the house occupied by Mr Robert Powell, opposite the Wesleyan chapel. Apparently a beam in the chimney caught fire (many cottage fires have started this way); the fire quickly spread to the cattle shed and stables behind the cottage. There was no fire brigade so all the able bodied men formed a bucket chain down the main street from the mill stream. Eventually a fire engine arrived, probably the one kept by the Acland family at Holnicote. It was a hand pumped machine, which needed three men each side pushing a bar up and down. The house and several other buildings were destroyed.

Luckily the two houses at the top of Sparkhayes Lane abutting on the Wesleyan chapel had just been built, so Mr Ridler of Sparkhayes Farm offered the top house to Mr Powell to rent as the first tenant. Lowerbourne was eventually rebuilt by the new owner, Mr Philip Arnold. He also had the grocers and drapers shop known as Lowerbourne House. Two new rows of cottages were built in Lowerbourne.

Today Porlock is a clean and tidy village, but it is only since 1960 that the cow sheds have gone from Sparkhayes Lane. The cows were regularly driven up the lane from the fields for milking while others were driven up the Porlock Weir road from the marsh to Court Place Farm.

At a court case in 1903 concerning pollution of a property in Porlock, the judge, in his summing up, described Porlock

Fire at Lowerbourne, 1900.

Flooding in the High Street, 1960.

Flooding in Hawkcombe, outside Japonica Cottage, October 1960.

thus: 'It has been said that life was a series of disappointments and disillusions, and certainly I have been disillusioned regarding Porlock. I have always thought it was a rural village with no smells about it, but the ozone from the ocean. But now, from what I have heard, it appears to be a very filthy village, one of the filthiest in Somersetshire'. Until 1889 there was no drainage of any kind whatever, and then only drainage for the 15 cottages of which they had heard. As far as the rest of the village went, it remained as it had been from the earliest days, and all the filth was thrown into the open stream. 'Fortunately it was not a town, in small villages people could endure a great deal of detrimental smell without danger to their health. But', he thought, 'few strangers who knew of this state of things would now be induced to go there in search of ocean breezes'.

The main stream is now quite clean, although it was very polluted and full of rubbish not so many years ago, despite notices to the effect that anyone throwing rubbish in the river would be fined £5.

In 1960 there was severe flooding in Porlock when the Hawkcombe Stream was blocked under the culvert of the bridge in the main street. The result was that the water came down Hawkcombe and Parson Street, flooding many shops and houses to a depth of up to 4 feet. The camp field in

Sparkhayes was like a lake with a waterfall coming off the field into Sparkhayes at the end of Furzeland Road. The water flowed like a river about 3 feet deep down Sparkhayes Lane to the Marsh. The sewer pipe which ran down the lane, and had been laid early in the century was left completely exposed, and the stones which had been washed out of the trench were deposited at the bottom of the lane. A new sewer was laid afterwards across the fields, parallel with the old sewer and a great deal of money was spent on flood protection measures, which included the widening of the Hawkcombe stream and deepening of the culvert under the main street.

The judge's comment in 1903 that people who lived in a small village could endure bad smells without detriment to health, did not ring true since prior to that time many children had died during epidemics in Porlock of diseases such as diptheria. It was for this reason that Porlock's first piped water supply came in 1876. Thirteen standpipes were placed at strategic points throughout the village e.g. outside Dovery Court, at the bottom of Lowerbourne, and opposite the Ship Inn.

One of the causes of pollution was a pack of hounds kept by Mr Henry Phelps at the back of Bridge House. The kennels drained into the stream, which was commonly called the 'Raggle'. These hounds were reputedly fox hounds but they were very unruly, and would chase cats and squirrels alike. One day they were passing through the village street, and an old lady had the top half of her hatch door open. A hound jumped in over and took a pound of butter. The lady shouted to the huntsman, 'Mr Phelps, that hound has stolen a pound of butter'. Quick as a flash Mr Phelps replied, 'Don't worry, missus, a bit of butter won't hurt him'.

The hounds were eventually sold to Mr Nicholas Snow of Oare, who was Master of the Hunt for 20 years. The pack was known as 'The Stars of the West', and were the forerunners of the Exmoor Fox Hounds.

9
PORLOCK MURDER CASE

Older people have often spoken of a murder which occurred in the village on Wednesday June 3rd 1914, just before 6 o'clock. It was when Harry Quartley shot Henry (Tacker) Pugsley. The illustrated Police News of June 11th, 1914 has a centre page artist's impression of the event, and reports as follows:

Village Tragedy. Startling Shooting Case at Porlock.

"The quiet West Somerset Village of Porlock has been dramatically disturbed by a shooting tragedy from behind a garden hedge, ending in the death of a resident, Henry Pugsley, and in the attempted suicide of the alleged assailant Henry Quartley, another villager, who is said to have borne a grudge against the victim. Some stray pellets from the gun with which the tragedy was committed struck a young woman named Alice Middleton but her injuries did not prove to be of a serious character. Pugsley's assailant subsequently attempted to shoot himself, but a local constable prevented him from doing so and took him to the Police Station.

Quartley is alleged to have said to a Superintendent Perry when he was arrested: 'I shot him, that is straight, that is the truth, so there is an end of it. How long did he live? Are you sure he is dead? Where did it touch him? Have you seen him?'.

A curious note, it is said, was found, scribbled on a scrap of paper in Quartley's pocket to this effect: 'I got no grievance against no-one else, only those two Pugsleys. They were the most dangerous crew I ever knew, and have only got to thank themselves, as they started it'.

He is fifty five years of age, unmarried, and by trade a mason, but he is possessed of private means left by his father. He owns house property, living with an unmarried sister in one of his own cottages, and he used the gun for sporting purposes."

Several people have told me their memories of the event. The Pugsleys lived in a cottage, one of two now demolished to make the car park opposite the Victoria Rooms in Parson Street, Sid Rawle remembered the incident very well, as he was coming out of the door of the billiard room opposite the Pugsleys' house when the shot was fired. Clifford Burgess was outside his father's baker's shop cleaning his new bicycle when the shot went off. Of course, the village policeman was soon on the scene, as were quite a number of spectators.

Pugsley had staggered indoors, and there died. Henry Quartley, who had fired over the garden wall, just up the road, then went to his own house, on the opposite side and went upstairs.

Constable Greedy's attention was diverted from the scene by the sound of a shot coming from Quartley's house. Greedy hurried in and went quickly upstairs; he found

Parson Street as it was, c. 1930-40. The Pugsley's thatched cottage and sweet shop on right. Quartley's cottage jutting out from left. Victoria Church Rooms on left.

Quartley's sister, Emily, in a bedroom. She was startled to see him, but warned him with, 'Look out Mr Greedy, else he will shoot you too'. Quartley stood in a curtained recess holding his gun. Mr Greedy jumped at him, knocking the gun from his hands and got him on his back on the floor, and shouted for help. Two men came up the stairs and the handcuffs were quickly on Quartley's wrists. Quartley had come close to killing himself, but had just missed his face,

the shot leaving a hole in the ceiling. The prisoner was quickly conveyed to Dunster Police Station, then the local headquarters, and from there to Exeter Prison. An inquest was held later at the Victoria Rooms, and a trial at the Somerset Assizes at Wells on October 20th.

It was a very short trial; Quartley insisted on his guilt, and all efforts to persuade him to accept counsel failed. The Judge had no alternative but to pronounce sentence of

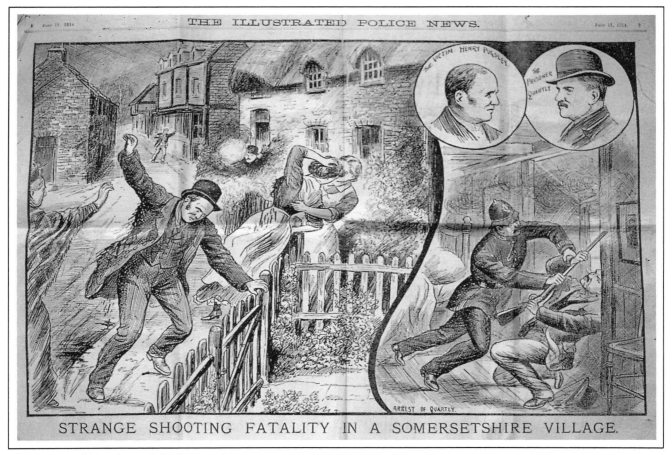

THE VICTIM- HENRY PUGSLEY

THE PRISONER QUARTLY

ARREST OF QUARTLY.

STRANGE SHOOTING FATALITY IN A SOMERSETSHIRE VILLAGE.

Artists impression of the murder scene. Police Gazette, 1914.

death. Henry Quartley was hanged at 8 am on Tuesday, November 10th.

P.C. Joseph Greedy's bravery in tackling an armed man was to be recognised by the award of the King's Police Medal. It seems that this terrible tragedy was the culmination of a much smaller quarrel during the previous year, which resulted in the Pugsleys taking Quartley to court for using indecent language in their house, and within hearing of the public highway. The case was dismissed because of lack of evidence, but Quartley, who together with his victim, had been well respected in the village, brooded over their quarrel, and things went from bad to worse until something snapped, and a terrible vengeance was taken.

10
PORLOCK HILL

Except for the fact that everyone driving up or down Porlock Hill realizes that it is very steep, most people today with their powerful cars and good brakes, take little notice of it, but it is world famed. Many older people will perhaps remember as I do that whenever you were away, maybe in the forces, you only had to mention that you were from Porlock, and almost everyone had heard of Porlock Hill. 'As steep as Porlock Hill?' was the West Country query when any steep piece of road was mentioned.

No-one knows when this route out of Porlock was first used and some local historians have suggested that Burley Lane from Parson Street was the old pack horse way out of Porlock towards Lynmouth and the hill farms. Collinson, writing in 1791, says of the Porlock area: 'Most of the roads are so poor and the fields so steep that no carriages of any kind can be used. All the crops are therefore carried in crooks on horses and the manure in wooden pots called dossels'. Robert Southey wrote of Porlock in 1797: 'This place is called in the neighbourhood; "The End of the World", all beyond is inaccessible to carriage, or even cart. A sort of sledge is used by the country people, resting upon two poles like cartshafts'.

In 1812 the condition of the road over Porlock Hill was such that the inhabitants of Porlock were presented at Quarter Sessions for failing to keep it in repair. The present way approaching the hill has always been known as Redway,

which could have meant just 'roadway', or it may have been because of the colour of the road when heavy rain brought the red soil down. At one time the people living in the cottages, killed and dressed their pigs at the side of the road; all the blood and waste would go down the stream, which was then an open gutter at the roadside. The hill wasn't tarred at the steepest part until 1930 and then as no steam roller could roll it in, it was done by hand, and then later still with a hand roller.

On a hunting day all the horses and spare horses with their grooms would be ridden up Porlock Hill; there were no horse boxes. Hunting was nearly as hard for the horses as it was for the deer. Sometimes over 100 riders would be out. Cart horses also used the hill. I well remember a shepherd from Court Place Farm riding up to tend his sheep at 'Holmbush'. He always cantered up the one in four part between the first and second bends.

The first stage coach went up the hill in 1843 as witnessed by Mr W. Symons, who, in his book *Early Methodism in West Somerset* says: 'It was my lot to charter the first stage coach to appear in Porlock, the occasion being a special excursion to Lynton. While waiting at the Ship, scores of inhabitants surrounded the coach and eagerly read the words painted on the exterior'. The four-in-hand coach never ceased to be one of the sights of Porlock, and long before it stopped in the 1920s the boys in the school playground used to crane their

The four-in-hand coach ascends Porlock Hill. Assisted by two leaders and a rider 1898.

The 1 in 4 section of Porlock Hill.

41

necks to see the coach turn the corner up to the Ship Inn, the coach horn having warned them of its coming.

I have often spoken to men, including my uncle, who as boys rode a leading horse up the hill. When the coach arrived at the Ship Inn, Mr Rook, the landlord would hire two horses as leaders from Mr David Ridler of Doverhay Farm, or Mr Isaac Burgess at the Bakery. When the coach was ready to leave, a boy would ride on one of the leaders, the coachman would whip up the leading horses – never his own – and away they went. Just before the first bend the coach would stop and the coachman would ask all the able bodied men to get out and walk. Then he would ask all the ladies under 40 to get out. This, of course would nearly empty the coach, ladies being fussy about revealing their age! The coach would then go up to just above the second bend and wait for the passengers. When all were aboard again they proceeded to the level just above Whitstones, where they would unhitch the leaders, thank the boy, who usually got some tip at this point. The coach then drove on whilst the boy took the leaders back to Porlock. On reaching Culbone Stables, or as it was then known Yearnor Moor, the horses were changed for the journey onward.

Many interesting tales have been told of the exploits of the boys who rode the leaders: my uncle, Clifford Burgess, told me that he used to leave a piece of old hoop iron under the heather at Whitstones, so that he could scrape off the lather from the horses before returning to Porlock. Maurice Hobbs, a nephew of Mr Rook at the Ship, while staying there was asked if he would like to ride a leader. Of course, he was eager to do so; his uncle said: 'Now whatever you do at Whitstones, don't get off the horse'. When they got to the top and unhitched the leaders, the coachman made a great fuss, and told the passengers how good the boy had been to bring them up safely over such a dangerous journey. They took it all in and feeling so grateful to be safe, started to throw money out for the boy. Some of the money fell to the ground, and Maurice, not wanting to miss any, jumped down to pick it up. The horses dashed off and made their way back to Porlock. Maurice had to walk all the way. Another story is told of a lad named 'Charlie' who was the butt of practical jokers; once when he rode a leader up, the other lads had put some shoe-maker's wax on the saddle. On arrival at Whitstones, Charlie was stuck fast in the saddle, and the story goes that they had to cut his breeches to get him off.

Coming down the hill the method of braking was to use a drag or drug shoe, which was a heavy iron fitted under the coach and attached by a chain. It was pushed under one of the back wheels which locked it, and the coach virtually slid down the hill, leaving a deep groove in the road.

In the early days of motoring the road was rough and in heavy rain just red mud, so if you just touched your brakes you were liable to slide. The council workers used to rake the road by hand each week. At the side was a deep ditch, and if you were not careful when passing another vehicle you could end up in it and have to be pulled out.

The first motor car to climb Porlock Hill was driven by G. B. Edge, for a wager in 1901 and the first motor cycle in 1909. A report reads:

A Motor Cycle Mounts Porlock Hill.

On the 23rd ult., this widely known hill, which is the steepest main-road hill in England, was successfully scaled by a motor-bicycle, Mr W Stone, of Taunton, having the honour of being the first motor cyclist to accomplish this feat. The hill has a gradient of about one in four for a considerable portion, and several very difficult corners, and rises about 1200 feet in three miles of its length. The surface is always rough owing to the coach traffic. Mr Stone was mounted on a Charter-Lea frame with 7hp. Peugeot Twin Engine and geared 4.5 to one. The time occupied on the ascent was but 6.5 minutes and the speed attained on such a gradient can only be described as marvellous especially as to the manner the engine picked up after each corner, the machine being pedal-less. The ascent was witnessed by Messrs King, Duddridge and Bennett of Taunton and several local people.

Trial on Porlock Hill, 1923.

In 1932 the Singer Car Company brought out a little car which was tested on Porlock Hill and was driven up and down 100 times, non–stop. The company named it the 'Porlock' model. The Daimler Car Company also tested their new cars loading them more and more until they broke down. After the Second World War Vauxhall and Bedford lorries were also tested in this way loaded with concrete blocks.

In spite of the gradient, there have been few fatal accidents on the hill. In 1950 Alfred Slade, who built the house on the first bend in 1930, went out to pick some flowers from his wall and a runaway car ran into him, and killed him. On another occasion a lady passenger died from a heart attack after descending the hill.

There have been, however, many other incidents when several people were injured. An armoured car ran away during the war, and hit the bank at the top of Conegar Orchard. A car ran away and finished up in Mr Frank

Norman's front room at Rose Cottage, and a crippled lady had to be lifted out through the car roof. Once in 1930 a Western National service bus from Lynmouth, driven by Arthur Priddle, stopped in the village and Mr Priddle went into the Post Office leaving his bus with the engine running. When the brake pads contracted after cooling off, the bus continued through the street with no driver. It went on over the bridge until it ran into Burgess's shop window. The first that Arthur Priddle knew of this was when a boy ran into the Post Office and said to him, 'Yer, thy bus 'ave run into Burgess's shop window'. Of course Arthur ran down the street to find his bus with its front in the shop, and the engine still running.

In the late 1950s a holiday coach ran away and went right through the village, the driver sounding the horn to warn other road users. The coach finally stopped near the War Memorial at Dunster Steep. Fortunately the road was clear; on the following day at precisely the same time, I spent several minutes sitting in the high street in a traffic jam. A coach driver once told me that he was taking a coach full of people up the hill, and they were quite worried as to whether the coach would make it to the top! The driver asked them all to lean forward, and this is what they did! On another occasion a coach ran away and finished up in a garden; in the coach sat 40 policemen!

For many years the AA and RAC had patrolmen with motorbike and sidecar on Porlock Hill every day, and they were kept busy with drivers needing assistance, as were the local garages who got the bulk of their business in the early days from Porlock Hill breakdowns. The RAC box was at the second bend, but has now been moved to 'Holmbush'. The AA box was, and still is, at Pitt Combe Head, and is a listed building, the only box of its kind in Somerset. One of the main jobs for the patrolmen was to keep the water butts filled, since so many cars boiled over.

Many early cars were gravity fed with petrol, and due to

A coal lorry overturns and sheds its load on Porlock Hill.

the steepness of the hill the petrol couldn't reach the carburettor. The answer was to drive up in reverse. Some of the first cars had a hand throttle on the steering column, and drivers would often run along beside their cars, having set the throttle, and steer from the outside, thus easing the weight in the car. Another problem was lorries with large loads such as hay, which could cause the front wheels to lift off the ground. In later days the biggest problem has been with larger lorries and articulators shedding their load on the road or caravans being too heavy for the car to pull. The driver tries to reverse; if he is lucky the caravan only gets stuck in the hedge; if unlucky, it turns over. Many people are still terrified of Porlock Hill and won't go up or down. In the early days some drivers were so frightened that local young men would offer to drive the car up or perhaps a gang of lads would push and keep them going. Once started, one or two would jump onto the running board of the car and ride to the top, usually getting a tip for their trouble.

The greatest excitement was at Easter time when the London-Lands End motor trials were on. A tea-room on the first bend was built in 1925 and Mrs Slade and her helpers stayed open all night on Good Friday as the spectators arrived. As many as 2000 would line the hill early on Saturday morning to watch the fun. The vehicles had to stop at the foot of the hill and then restart. Before the hill was tarred in 1929, the stones would fly out from under the driving wheels. After 1931 the motor-cycles and sidecars and three wheelers all had to do Doverhay Hill as a timed circuit, Porlock Hill being now too easy for them. After going up Doverhay to Woodcocks Ley (the track is now overgrown) they returned via West Luccombe, then on again to Porlock and up Porlock Hill.

During the 1950s the Milk Marketing Board ran their round-Britain race for professional cyclists. One stage of the race was from Weston-Super-Mare to Ilfracombe. I stood amongst other spectators on the bank at the second bend and we saw the cyclists come down Dunster Steep in a bunch, around the corner by the Royal Oak, and then by the Ship Inn. They soon appeared all cycling up the hill, except one, who ran all the way up with his bike on his shoulder. In the evening I bought a paper to read the results. The first two

Clearing snow on Porlock Hill, 1940.

had arrived at Ilfracombe with only a wheel distance between them after a ride of about 80 miles.

Snow and ice are a great problem on Porlock Hill. At one time people didn't use their cars so much in winter, and local people seldom ventured over Porlock Hill for fear of getting caught in snow. But now with car heaters more efficient, they use them much more. Drifts can be up to 15 feet deep on the top, and it is usual to put grit and salt down at the first sign of snow. There have been years when deep snow means snow ploughs trying to clear it as far as County Gate, where they hope to meet the Devon clearing team. The only trouble is that the snow will often come again the next night and high winds will blow it off the moor and back into the road. In the 1920s and 30s shovels would be used by gangs of workmen, but after the war snow ploughs and bulldozers were used. Snow was cut through, and I have seen it cut like cheese at Oare Post, about 12 feet in depth with a wall of snow ahead.

In 1963 the road was closed for eight weeks and cars were completely buried near the AA box. Traffic to Barnstaple had to take the southern route via South Molton. The cost to the Highway Authority was enormous, as it was also to the telephone company. Until the wires were put underground on Porlock Hill they often blew down in high gales just at the time when people were most isolated. In snow storms traders have done their utmost to keep the hill farmers' families and villagers of Oare and Brendon supplied with meat, bread and groceries, sometimes riding ponies out when it was impossible to take a van. One local doctor used skis to go to a patient at Oare. When an old lady died at Oareford and her body had to be brought to Porlock for burial, the hill was impassable, but two men were sent with a lorry up the Toll Road. They struggled up as far as Westcott Brake, but could go no further. So they waited until they saw the heads of two horses coming towards them through the deep snow; it was a farmer with a horse drawn cart with the coffin, which was then taken back to Porlock.

In recent years R.A.F. rescue helicopters have been used in emergencies, and so many problems have been easily solved. The people of Exmoor now have not so much fear of isolation, and Porlock Hill is no longer the terror that it once was, but it still must be treated with respect.

Often in summer-time in the village, the smell of burning rubber is quite sickening. This is, of course, brake rubber, for cars stop when there is a traffic holdup with smoke pouring from their brakes. The wise driver knows that bottom gear is best for Porlock Hill, whereas many ignore the warning signs, not thinking that they have not only the family, but all their luggage as well; a tremendous weight in a car for such a hill.

In the 1950s or '60s an 'escape' road was made at the second bend, in order that cars out of control could be driven into the road where deep sand would stop them immediately. It is amazing how many people park vehicles, stand and watch the traffic or even picnic on the sand there.

11
THE TOLL ROAD AND PARKS

Parks were created by great landowners only under a licence from the king, for the purpose of hunting deer and other game on their own lands, the forest being the king's hunting preserve. Porlock Parks were set out in the 1300s during Sir Nigel Loring's lordship. Bounded by a wall and ditch surmounted by a fence, they have been part of the Porlock Estate ever since, and the wall and ditch can still be seen at the top of the woods. The present owner is Mr Blathwayt.

George Winter bought Dyrham in Gloucestershire in 1571. He married Anne Brayne of Bristol, and their eldest son, John (who sailed with Sir Francis Drake), married Mary Brouncker of Erlestoke, Wiltshire. His son, Sir George Winter, succeeded him in 1619 and married Mary, daughter of Edward Rogers of Cannington, Somerset, whose dowry was the Porlock Manor Estate. When Sir George Winter died in 1638, his son John was only 16. He later married Frances, the daughter of Thomas Gerard of Trent. Their daughter, Mary, was their only child, and she on December 23rd 1686 married William Blathwayt, Secretary of State to William III, who thus became the owner of Dyrham and Porlock.

The family visited Porlock frequently but did not live here. The first resident was Frances, widow of Mr Blathwayt the fourth and re-married to Admiral Douglas. They lived from 1824 in what is now the Cottage Hotel at Porlock Weir. The family home was later moved to West Porlock where a new house was built c.1920, the stone being quarried behind the house. West Porlock House is now divided into flats.

The old manor house of Porlock was on the site of Court Place Farm. The old house was destroyed by fire sometime in the early 1800s. The Manor Court was held at Court Place and when the Lord of the Manor stopped living there, it became the residence of the farmer of the demesne lands. The site chosen for the lord's house was ideal, in a central position and overlooking almost all of the land in the lower part of the estate. The Manor Pound is still below the house, and the Manor Mill only a few hundred yards down the street. When the men of the town went to the Butt Garden for their archery practice, as they were obliged to do in the time of Henry VIII, they could be watched by the lord or his bailiff from the windows of the house. (The Butt Garden was a meadow near the present fire station).

In about 1840 Mr Blathwayt, the then Lord of the Manor, decided to build a new road, a scenic drive being the intention rather than the avoidance of Porlock Hill. This started from just above the Ship Inn, and followed an easier gradient for 4.5 miles to Pitt Combe Head. It was dug out manually, no doubt giving work during the depressed times after the Napoleonic Wars. Mr Blathwayt went out in a boat with a fisherman from Porlock Weir to view and plan the course of the road. He also employed a French engineer. The route needed several bridges over, culverts under the

A hairpin bend on Porlock Toll Road.

steep combes, and much excavation. It cut through existing boundary and field walls. It also cut across the old track from Porlockford to Birchanger Farm.

At first the road was just a rough track used by horses; The earliest list of charges is dated August 12th, 1857. Porlock New Road. Turnpike accounts:

	s.	d.
Horse and Gig		6
Horse and Cart		4
Carriage and 2 horses	1	0
Carriage and pair	1	0
Coach	1	6
Horse		1
Waggon		9
Donkey		3
Bus and 4 horses	1	6
Machine and 3 horses		9
Engine and 3 horses		9

It is interesting to see that a donkey was 3d., whereas a horse was only 1d. It can only be assumed that a donkey carried a load, while a horse was usually used for pleasure, or by a farmer going home, or out on business.

Pine trees were planted and are still to be seen marking the line of the road. The natural oaks and ash are interspersed with chestnut and walnut trees. Later conifer plantations have been felled and replanted.

Taking the toll.

The first tolls were taken at the Ship Inn and there used to be a gate across at the bottom of the road, opposite the present village hall. In quiet times a boy would run out from the Ship Inn to take the toll, but on busy days in summer-time, or on a hunting day, he would stay at the gate.

In 1924 the toll houses were built at the half way point, and the gate at Porlock taken away. The stone for the houses came partly from the deserted Keepers Cottage nearby, at the top of the wood above Aller Park. Little is to be seen there now except the garden wall and part of the floor of the cottage. There is one odd window of leaded glass in one of the toll cottages which came from the Keepers Cottage.

With the advent of motor cars, the road was used a good deal and many people today prefer to pay a toll rather than risk Porlock Hill. In my younger days everyone referred to the road as the New Road, rather than the Toll Road. The

New Road has been a great asset to Porlock as it makes a lovely walk especially at quiet times. The scenery for walker and motorist alike, especially on the downward journey, makes it one of the most beautiful routes in the area.

West Porlock, the Parks and toll houses from the Marsh.

12
WEST PORLOCK

The road from Porlock to the harbour at Porlock Weir passes through the hamlet of West Porlock.

There are some lovely old cottages, many modernised, but still retaining the old features. The old door of one cottage, now replaced, had roughly carved into it a heart with an arrow through it, believed to have been a sign to ward off witches. During alterations at Dunns Court two lovely inglenook fireplaces were opened up as well as an old faggot oven. A hiding place for valuables was found in the stone floor where a mat would have covered it. The outbuildings had stalls for carthorses, being the Manor Farm at one time.

At the top of the steep on the left is Fern Cottage, part of an old house, which sometime in the last century was used as a public house, the Live and Let Live. The last landlady was a Mrs Burgess, whose descendants told me that it was an ale house. The old lady only had a licence to sell ale but the authorities found out she was selling spirits and consequently she lost her licence. One wonders if the spirits were obtained legally, or if they were smuggled in.

The Cook family, who lived at the Live and Let Live in my memory, had, for two generations, collected ferns, which were gathered under a licence from both the Blathwayt and Lovelace families, from the Parks and Culbone Woods. The ferns were made up into circular bundles carefully laid with stalks outwards (these were true ferns, not bracken). The bundles were then covered in hessian, and the carrier would pick them up and take them to Minehead station, where they would be sent to London for use by fishmongers, who placed them under fish on the marble slabs. Fishmongers still use ferns, but they are not real, only plastic!

Further along the road is the old forge, now cleverly converted to a private dwelling. The last blacksmith was Mr Jack Moggridge, who followed his father at the forge. The usual smithing jobs were carried out there, including shoeing. There in the yard is a little thatched building, where Mr Moggridge used to keep his cider; it was originally the village lock-up. Tradition has it, although there is no written record, that it was used by the village constable to lock up suspected rebels in the Monmouth rebellion pending transfer to Judge Jeffrey's assizes; also, later on, seamen captured from the French and Spanish privateers.

At the west end of the hamlet, the last cottage on the left has a large leaded window and this was the little shop and workshop of the leather craftsman, Mr Philip Burgess. Originally he was in the building trade and re-shingled the church steeple in 1890, fixing up a little platform which could be hauled up and down to work from. He learnt embossed leather work in a class for boys started by a Miss Baker at Chapel Knap and became so good at this work that he eventually set up business. Some of his work can be seen in the area, notably the Angels on the Reredos in Selworthy Church, and a frieze of a hunting scene around a room at

Old cottages West Porlock. Formerly the Live and Let Live.

Bossington Place, originally New Place, built by Sir Charles Chadwyck-Healey.

On one occasion a gentleman called at his shop and looking around became interested in his work. He asked if Mr Burgess could copy an old worn leather seat. A few days later the chair cover arrived with the pattern so worn that it was difficult to follow. Mr Burgess put a lot of time and trouble into this work and when it was finished sent it, together with the old cover to the address given somewhere in the City of London. At last a letter came with a good cheque inside. The gentleman had written: 'We have examined your work alongside the original, and are unanimously of the opinion it is the better work of the two. The old piece was taken from a chair in the chancel of St Paul's Cathedral. Yours is now in its place, and I hope will remain there for some hundreds of years'.

Between West Porlock and Porlockford was once Gaptree Orchard. The Gaptree was blown down during the 1950s and fell across the road. This spot was said to be haunted by the ghost of Nelly Carew. She was a character in *Katerfelto*, a novel by G. J. Whyte-Melville who stayed at Porlockford during which time he soaked up the atmosphere of the area, and wrote the novel, in which he well describes the life and scenery of Porlock Bay and Exmoor.

Porlockford House was built on the site of a previous house, and has been a riding centre for many years. The ford, of course, is now bridged and the stream flows under the road near the entrance to the house. Just a short way up into the woods is the village hut, much used by the past residents of Porlock Weir and West Porlock for social events, dances, meetings etc. The building was originally an army building from the First World War, and is still in use.

13
PORLOCK WEIR

Porlock Weir has been essential to the economy of Porlock for centuries. We can only surmise that the first harbour was built by the fourteenth century, as, according to the bailiff of Brendon's accounts of 1422/23: 'paid to Robert Godde (the lady's receiver) for the repair of the Weir at West Porlock'. And in 1426: '1 heifer paid to Robert Godde – clerk – for the making of the Weir at Porlock'. The name 'Weir' puzzles people as there is no sizeable river or a weir on it. There are other meanings of the word; it can be a fishing weir, where posts were fixed at low water level to hold nets for trapping fish, possibly salmon. R. D. Blackmore in *Lorna Doone* refers to Lynmouth Weir, and we know that this method of fishing has been used along the Bristol Channel coast for years. A weir is also a place for building boats, and for careening the hulls (scraping off the barnacles). Some believe that Worthy Water once entered the harbour but it made a new course after a severe flood many years ago.

The first harbour would have been quite crude. Early photographs and the ordnance survey map of 1888 show a bridge further up the dock than at present. Records show that money was spent from time to time on the dock and lock gates. The lock gates, which replaced the previous wooden ones, were erected about 1913 and were constructed away from Porlock. There are similar ones in the old docks at Cardiff. The opening of the new dock was celebrated by an official ceremony, when all the local people turned out. Bunting decorated the boats; ketches and also trows which were mainly used on the River Severn and the upper reaches of Channel.

At one time quite sizable vessels, up to 100 tons, came into Porlock Weir – men would have to slide back the bridge by pulling on ropes. As a boy I often watched the unloading of coal; a pulley worked by a donkey engine in the vessel was used. The coal was lifted from the hold in maunds (double handled wicker baskets). Much of the coal was stored in the yard and sheds beside the harbour house (now 'Pieces of Eight'), from where it was delivered by horse and cart and later by lorries. In 1875 there was also a brick and tile company beside the inner harbour.

There used to be several fishing families. I remember Preston and Arthur Ley, and Jack Ridler who had fishing boats. Before them were the Pugsley and Pollard brothers, the Perkins and a Mr Ward. Often I have seen Preston Ley out in the bay on a cold winter's day fishing with drift nets for herring.

Porlock Weir herrings were very popular, being much fresher than those brought down from Great Yarmouth. There are several reasons why the herrings have declined in numbers in the Bristol Channel; overfishing in the Channel approaches and pollution are just two. For hundreds of years boats went out for herrings from Minehead, Porlock

The 'Elizabeth Anne' and a smaller smack, Porlock Weir, 1884. Note limestone which has been unloaded over the side of vessels.

Mending sails, 1880. Back to camera Jack Pugsley, in bowler hat Jim Pulsford, facing camera Tom Sparks. Note wooden footbridge on left.

Sunday School outing to Porlock Weir, c.1890-95. Porlock band in attendance in their new 'dapper' uniforms. Note fish market, now a car park.

Weir, Lynmouth and other parts of North Devon. The fish would be sold from the quays and local shops, or delivered by dealers around the villages. When there were plenty, some would be salted down in barrels. (The saltern at Porlock Weir is now a carpenter's workshop). If there was still a surplus, it was known for the fish to be sent to Bossington for spreading on the land as fertilizer.

The fish market at Porlock Weir is seen on early photographs situated opposite the Anchor Hotel on the edge of the present car park. Here the fishermen sold their catch until the turn of the twentieth century. The herrings were in maunds or boxes, and while the joulers (ie dealers) were haggling over the price, the men would be 'telling up the catch'. Herrings were sold in long hundreds, the method of

Net making. Mrs Ann Pollard making a net for the fishermen, c.1880.

counting thus: two men would count out in threes, each would pick up three herrings in turn and count 'wan, two, dree' and so on up to 40, ie 120 herrings. Then at the next three the men would say 'warp and tail' and one herring would be placed on the ground. Then the counting would be repeated as many times as necessary until the buyer had enough hundreds. The one on the ground representing each long hundred could easily be counted for example: if there were five herrings on the ground, there were five long hundred in the buyer's box or basket. The three herrings for 'warp and tail' were extra, I am told, for paying any turnpike tolls on the buyer's journey. When herrings were plentiful at that time, they were sold for 2s.6d. a hundred.

At the point where the lower road from Porlock begins its

run alongside the beach, is the site of the former 'bark-house'. Trees were felled and stripped in the woods and the bark stored here for transporting to the tanyard at Porlock. There were more fields on the seaward side of the barkshed, but they were gradually swept away by erosion and the road itself is only preserved by the massive concrete walling on either side of the steps down to the beach.

A map of Porlock dated 1710 shows an oyster bed in Porlock Bay. Oysters were dredged for many years on both sides of the Channel, but the beds shifted. In the mid-nineteenth century, Porlock beds proved poor and c.1870, Noah and William Pollard's uncle and his crew were dredging for oysters off the Mumbles, but with little success. Returning to Porlock they decided to try their luck once more in Porlock Bay. To their astonishment they made a wonderful catch, and decided to continue oyster fishing. Soon an average catch was 1200 per day. The dredge was towed behind their sailing boat on a long line. It had a cutting edge of iron about 1 metre long, known as the sword and the oysters were dragged off the sea bottom into a type of net made of chain link. Then the net would be hauled up and tipped into the boat. The oysters were kept in a walled-in area known as a perch where the tides left them at low water. They remained in the perch in bags of 600 until needed. Most of the oysters were sent to Bristol.

The oyster perch still remains at Porlock Weir right opposite the two houses built for William and Noah Pollard, named 'Oyster Perch' and 'Mizpah' (the second a biblical name meaning 'watch-tower'). Whether there are still oysters in Porlock Bay is debatable as the waters are very polluted nowadays. It used to be said that the oyster fishing finished when boats from Whitstable and Colchester came from the East Coast and dredged the oyster beds in order to replenish their stocks. As there was no law to prevent them, all the Pollard brothers could do was look helplessly on.

The brothers Pollard were not only fishermen, but boat builders too. The indentures of Noah Pollard are still held by his grandson, Fenwick. Boats were built at Porlock Weir, and in 1723 there was a charge of '3 shillings upon every boat, and 6 shillings on every barque built upon the lords waste'. There exists a very comprehensive list of tolls

Inner basin, Porlock Weir. Note old lime kiln with Ashley Combe House in the distance.

payable to the lord of the manor. This gives the harbour dues for imports and exports of 78 different commodities including fish and fruit and even 1 penny for every dozen pair of stockings.

In more recent times many a boat was laid up and left to rot in the inner harbour. Others were converted to pleasure cruisers; one, 'Breeze' lay beside the dock for many years, seldom used. She has now returned from Barry where her present owner had her rebuilt. The 'Breeze' was formerly a Bristol Channel Pilot Cutter of 19 tons. Built in 1887 at Pill she is the last of the Transom Stern Pilot Cutters.

Just after the Second World War a sailing club was formed at Porlock Weir which ran very successfully for several years. New 18 foot sailing dinghies were popular, some designed and built by Uffa Fox, of Cowes fame, and some from Kimbers yard at Highbridge. Porlock Weir boats competed in many of the Bristol Channel races off the Mumbles, Barry and Weston. The club, disbanded for a number of years, has now reformed.

Boat trips around the bay were once very popular and provided extra income when the herring season had finished. Some fishermen's wives let rooms for boarding or bed and breakfast. Some served teas or made up trays of tea for visitors to take to the beach. Sea swimming was very

Porlock Weir Regatta, 1913.

popular when the weather was good and water polo was played in the harbour for a few seasons.

The three hotels were also kept busy, even more so since the increase of motor traffic. At the turn of the century the landlord at the Anchor Hotel was Mr James Goddard. The hotel was mainly used by guests for the hunting season. Mr Goddard kept up to 25 horses and ran a horse bus to carry passengers from and to the station at Minehead for a fare of 1s.6d. Porlock Weir was always an attraction at high tides, especially on the very high tides in September. I have seen the yard of the Ship Inn full of sea water and have watched the landlord, Bernard Perkins, watch in hand, standing at the door of the bar. The water was lapping the step, but he didn't even put a sandbag across. He knew the time of the tide and sure enough, within a few minutes, the water started to recede.

That was a fairly quiet evening tide but there are occasions when some of the cottages get flooded. There was the famous time in 1910 which folk talked about for many years and referred to as the 'tidal wave' or the 'wash out' at Porlock Weir. On that occasion much structural damage was done and the road leading to the village was covered in stones. The hedge on the other side of the road was partially washed away. The sea came halfway up the gardens of 'Oyster Perch', and 'Mizpah' and the cottages at Gibralter, which back on to the beach were all flooded. A Miss Pugsley was to be married and her wedding cake was on the sitting room table. Both table and cake floated to the ceiling and then were submerged in sea water. Mr Stenner, the baker, quickly replaced the cake. Everyone had to spend the night in the church at the top of Lane Head. Jim Sparkes, who was a boy at the time, nearly lost his life when a wave swept into the bedroom at Beach Cottage and on going back, dragged him to the bedroom window. He had a lucky escape as Mr Pollard caught and held him.

A man who lived at Porlock Weir once told me that the Worthy Stream used to run into Porlock Weir harbour, but during a great storm it broke through to make a new outlet to the sea, where it still is. The story was probably passed on for generations, and it is on record that on October 13th, 1625 there was a great flood, as there is also recorded a

Aftermath of great storm, 1910.

Porlock Weir. The lock gates closed for sluicing.

number of persons making a petition to Quarter Sessions at Wells on July 11th 1626, signed by two Magistrates, the Minister and 27 residents of Porlock. The victim of this flood was 'Grace Mogridge of Porlock, Widow, whose house and grounds were lying neare the sea by a small lake, whose discent is from a very steepe woodie mountayne'. The most likely place of this is at the foot of Worthy Combe. It appears that poor Grace Mogridge's dwelling house, out-houses, fishing equipment, garden, and two acres of hops etc. were washed into the sea, to the total value of £200 and upwards. It was decided at the sessions to advance 'the poor woman £6-13s-4d towards her relief in this her extremitie'.

The beach continually shifts at Porlock Weir, necessitat-ing the making of groins or timber hedges. The harbour used to be sluiced through a tunnel (no longer used) the sluice being controlled from a stone building on the quay. The lock gates would be closed and then opened for sluicing, but this was not very satisfactory because the flow of water went in too much of an easterly direction. Sometimes these days a mechanical digger is used. At Porlockford the sea has encroached on the land considerably and the sea wall had to be strengthened early in the 1950s.

The harbour was too small to accommodate large vessels. One top sail schooner, the 'Florence Muspratt' of 78 tons, was owned by Mr Harry Manley who kept the grocer's shop at the Weir. The ship had too great a draught to enter the

Ashley Combe House.

harbour, but traded up and down the Channel and beyond. As she sailed past Porlock Weir, Mr Manley would point her out with pride, and she always dipped her ensign on passing her owner's port. The vessel was built at Burton Struther in Lincolnshire in 1869. She was commandeered for war service in 1914. On September 5th 1917 whilst under command of Capt. Jack Redd she sailed from St Malo for Newport in ballast, to pick up coal. She was fired on by a German submarine, one member of the crew was killed, the captain and two others took to the boat, and a few minutes later she sank. The surviving crew were picked up by a French patrol boat and came safely home.

Other Porlock Weir craft were the 'Fanny', built in Aberthaw in 1753, owned by John Moore, and then several generations of the Pulsford family. She traded between South Wales and Minehead, and was wrecked at Barry in 1883. William Pulsford built his own smack 'John and William', at the back of the harbour in 1858. The Pollard Brothers built the 'Rosa'. Other boats were The 'Two Sisters' of William Pollard; John Perkin's 'Betsy' and John Red's 'Caerleon', 'Eleanor Mary' and 'Elizabeth Anne'. Later Tom Ley came from Combe Martin with his 'Mistletoe' and settled at Porlock Weir where his sons, grandsons, and great grandson carried on the tradition of small boat fishing. My own memories are of the coal boats, such as the 'Bessie Clarke' and the 'Democrat' of Barnstaple.

During the nineteenth century many of the cargoes were of culm from Swansea, coal from Penarth or limestone from Barry. Other imports were salt, flour and groceries. Pit props were the main export to South Wales and Bristol; also brick cargoes to Bristol and in summer brick and bark to Penzance.

Beyond Porlock Weir lies Worthy, a lovely house parts being very old. We know there was a house at Worthy as early as the reign of Edward I. The estate, which once consisted of a farm and about 40 acres of land was frequently called Worthy Manor, but there is no known evidence that it ever was entitled to be described as a manor using the word in the technical sense.

In the woods above Worthy on the far side of the combe are the ruins of Ashley Combe House, formerly Ashley Combe Lodge. The house was demolished about 1960. It is believed that a house was on the site in the seventeenth century. It was Lord King, the 8th Baron (later to become the first Lord Lovelace), who improved and extended the house and created the Italian gardens. The house was built in the style of an Italian castle and there were several tunnels in the grounds, large enough for traders' vehicles to approach the house unseen. Many trees were planted in the grounds. The Lovelace family owned Yearnor, Culbone, Sparkhayes and Bratton, near Minehead. The view from the house was magnificent, looking over Porlock Weir and across the bay. Lord King married Ada, the daughter of Lord Byron.

Countess Ada Lovelace is one of the few women to figure in computing history. She was a gifted mathematician who understood Charles Babbage's Analytical Engine and wrote some of the best accounts of how it worked. She even devised programs for it and was thus the world's first computer programmer.

Rockford Cottage, a quarter of a mile beyond Gore Point, was a boathouse with access through the woods to Ashley Combe House. It was described on summer boat trips as a 'smuggler's cottage' and certainly was well-sited for such use. Unfortunately the path and almost all of the cottage have disappeared due to the continuous landslips in the Culbone Woods.

I wonder if the Porlock Weir people saw the French Ships coming up the Channel in 1797, with a force, many of whom were released convicts, intending to land at Bristol and march on London. They were sighted at Ilfracombe, where an old lady stood on the cliff beating a kettle drum as a warning. However, when in sight of Porlock, the wind turned contrary, so the ships changed course, sailed down Channel and around St David's Head to land at Fishguard. Here they were soon rounded up by the inhabitants and the Castle Martin yeomanry.

14
SOME VILLAGE CHARACTERS

Mr Bill Court used to drive a horse and cart for Cooksleys the builders, and one of his regular jobs was bringing up stones from Bossington Beach. One day he got to the bottom of Bush Steep on his way to Porlock, when he met two gentlemen who were on holiday from London. One of them, I suspect, thought: 'Here's a countryman we can have some fun with', so he said, 'Excuse me, my man! have you seen a cartload of monkeys passing this way?'. Mr Court scratched his head and thought. Then he said: 'No sir; why? 'Have you two fell off?'. The visitors were taken aback by this quick witted reply. One said to Mr Court: 'Which pub do you patronize?' to which came the reply 'The Royal Oak'. The result of course, a free drink or two that evening.

Once in the bar of the Ship Inn, Porlock Weir, a holidaymaker asked one of the locals, Bob Davis, 'What do you do here to pass the time during the winter when all the visitors have gone home?'. 'Oh', says Bob, 'We 'aves a lovely time, we just sits yer and laughs and laughs and laughs'. 'Good Lord', says the visitor, 'Whatever do you laugh about?'. 'Why sir', says Bob, 'We laughs at all you silly B...s that come down yer in the summer'.

Bob Davis was a very clever man with his hands. He lived in a little cottage at Porlock Weir which is now named 'Bob's Cottage'. Although he could barely read or write, he was very good at repairing clocks. His little room was full of them. He could also true up a buckled bicycle wheel. He made wooden furniture, sails for a boat, and he even made a violin once, and played it. It is said he once made a boat in his house but couldn't get it out of the door, so he had to break it up again. I was once talking to another Porlock character, Charlie Powell, and I said that Bob Davis was a very clever man. 'Oh yes', says Charlie, 'Bob Davis is a well educated man, but it's a pity he can't read or write'.

Charlie used to blow the church organ at one time, when Mr Sidney Cooksley was the organist. One Sunday Charlie said: 'You can play what you like, Mr Cooksley, I'm going to blow for Rock of Ages.' Another story concerning Charlie I heard only recently. It came from a man who sang in the church choir when he was a boy. The boys collected about 20 snails from the churchyard, and put them on Charlie's seat by the organ. They hoped to have a laugh, but, fortunately for Charlie, the organist came first, and sat down to change his shoes, and sat on the snails instead.

Of course some stories are true and can be vouched for, while others are somewhat 'far fetched' as we used to say; some get added to by the better story tellers, so you need to take them with a 'pinch of salt'.

One story started during the last war. White lines were painted in the middle of the road so drivers could see the line of the road during the black-out. Some found the best way to drive was to straddle the line and when you saw another light approaching you moved to the left. Remember there was nothing like the amount of traffic that there is today. One night a Porlock resident drove home from Minehead, following the white line intently until he could go no further. He had arrived at the posts in the road outside the Anchor Hotel at Porlock Weir, without realizing he'd driven straight through Porlock!

There were, of course, practical jokers always up to tricks for the fun of it. Young lads would often be sent on errands with notes telling the receiver to send him on further, or perhaps they were sent to the leather shop for strap oil! There they would be given a slap with a leather strap. The school boys would tie two door knockers together, knock on one door, and when it was answered the other knocker would lift, and so it would go on. One day at West Porlock the boys put a sack of bricks over the chimney of the blacksmith's shop. Of course, the shop became very smoky and Jack Moggridge, the blacksmith, said: 'Phew, smoke's flying low, there must be rain about' When he realized that the chimney was blocked he poked a rod up the chimney and dislodged the sack, which came down through the roof.

An old lady, Lizzie Jarvis, lived in a cottage next to the school playground. The boys would throw stones from the playground and try to get them down her chimney. One day she went into the school to complain with two stones in her frying pan.

There was a man called Jim Pulsford at Porlock Weir and people said he was a 'proper scamp'. One day, a lady who lived at Worthy Manor lost one of her peacocks, so she offered a reward to anyone who found it. Jim Pugsley was working in the woods above Worthy and from the other side of the combe Jim Pulsford saw him catch the lost peacock. Quick as a flash Jim Pulsford went down and knocked on the door of Worthy Manor, spoke to the lady, and said: 'It's alright Ma'am, we've caught the peacock, Jim Pugsley will be bringing him down in a few minutes'. 'Oh thank you', said the lady, 'here's you reward'. Off went Pulsford with the money. On another occasion Pulsford again went off with the money. He took a party of chaps carol singing to Ashley Combe. There was at that time a regular village choir led by 'Tinker' Huish, the Porlock blacksmith. They used to go around the district each year, and were known as 'Tinker's

Choir'. Pulsford got to Ashley Combe where his choir sang for a few minutes. Lady Lovelace came out and asked them if they were 'Tinker's Choir', 'Oh yes', said Pulsford. So she gave them the money and off they went. It can be imagined what was said when later the real 'Tinker's Choir' turned up at Ashley Combe and began to sing.

The mode of speech was very different among village people even when I was a boy. One day I was sent with a pair of bellows for repair to Tinker Huish. Several days later I met Tinker in the Drang and he said: 'Yer, I've mend thee bellas'. 'Pardon', I said. 'I've mend thee bellas', he said. Three times he said this before I understood what he meant! 'I've mended your bellows'.

Mr Isaac Burgess was delivering bread to the Ship Inn at Porlock, when a certain man who had recently taken up preaching in the Methodist Church was in the bar for a drink. On seeing Mr Burgess approaching and knowing that he was not only a keen Methodist, but also a teetotaller (not all were) the man said to Mr William Rook, the landlord: 'What shall I do, Mr Rook'. 'Hide in that cupboard', said Mr Rook. So the man stepped inside the cupboard. Mr Burgess entered and asked how much bread. 'A couple of loaves', said Mr Rook, 'put them in that cupboard there, don't leave them on the bar'. Whereupon Mr Burgess opened the cupboard door, and there was the nameless gentleman inside with a glass of beer in his hand.

Until a few years ago there were two bakers in the village; Burgess's and Stenner's. This story concerns Mr Walter Stenner, who was having difficulty in getting his money at one house. One day he called with the bread, and after putting it on the table, the daughter of the house who was there said: 'Mother can't pay today, she's gone to Minehead'. 'Oh,' said Mr Stenner, 'next time she goes, tell her to take her feet with her'. The lady had hidden behind a curtain and the toes of her shoes were showing underneath.

A Porlock lady used to tell a tale of a local preacher who went to preach at Wheddon Cross before there was a chapel there. He stood on top of a barrel to preach, and being rather a ranter he started to get excited and began to shout 'The righteous shall rise up, and the wicked shall go down to hell', wherewith the top of the barrel caved in and down he went.

Old Charlie went up to Hacketty Way House and asked Mr Fairchild, the head gardener, for some bedding plants. 'How many do you want, Charlie?', said Mr Fairchild. 'Oh only two or three', says Charlie, 'but mix 'em up a bit, will'ee'.

Children get strange ideas. At Porlock school some children were discussing the 'Trow Pool', which is opposite the Anchor Hotel at Porlock Weir. A boy who lived at Porlock Weir said it was bottomless; he knew it was bottomless because his father had helped to dig it! Another young boy from Porlock Weir went to sea in a local ketch. Of course his father was very proud of him and when asked how the boy was getting on, he said: 'He's doing very well, he's been to foreign parts'. 'Foreign parts?', was the question. 'Oh 'ees, Lynmouth and Cardiff and about'.

A chimney sweep sweeping a chimney at the Anchor Hotel asked Jim Pulsford to give him a shout when the brush came out at the top. He kept putting on more rods and he shouted to Jim asking if the brush was up? 'No', said Jim, so more rods were put on. The sweep couldn't understand why Jim hadn't shouted! So the sweep shouted again to Jim and when there was no reply he went outside; Jim had disappeared and the brush was hanging down over the roof nearly to the road.

Some young men played a joke one night when they hung up a horn lantern from the flag pole outside the Anchor Hotel at Porlock Weir. Two old chaps came out from the Ship Inn (they had had a drop too much!) One looked up at the light, and said: 'Caw, I've never seen the moon looking so dirty.' 'No', said the other, 'and I've never seen 'en out north before!'

One day I learned that a shark had been washed up on the beach at Porlock Weir. I saw my friend Ernie Pollard and enquired: 'I hear there's a shark at Porlock Weir'. Quick as a flash he laughed as he replied; 'Ah, and I reckon there's a few up Porlock too'.

When Mr Goddard kept the Anchor Hotel at the end of the last century, he had a scarecrow put up in one of the fields near the hotel. A local man went up there, saw the scarecrow, thought its clothes were better than his own, so he changed clothes with the scarecrow and went on his way.

Sometimes in excitement words are put backwards. A man at Luccombe one day, saw a lady repairing her fence and not making a very good job of it. He offered to help: 'Don't worry missus', he said, 'give us half a dozen hammers and a nail, and I'll soon mend thee fence'.

Ted Kent was an undertaker who lived at Allerford. He went to visit a friend who was ill and lived on Selworthy Green. Whilst there he said to the friend: 'Well I may as well run the tape over 'ee while I'm yer!' The same man took a party of carol singers out one Christmas and they sang at the home of the Stenner family who kept the Allerford Laundry at Brandish Street (now demolished). When they had sung a few carols they were invited inside for refreshments. Miss Stenner handed round some mince pies which everyone enjoyed, so Mr Kent said: 'Nice mince pies, Miss Stenner'. And turning to his friends, he said: 'Would you chaps like some more?'. Miss Stenner was obliged to bring out more.

It is hard to visualise what life was like and how it differed from today. For example, we are used to all the summer traffic and tourists. I was told this next story by Mr Arthur Smith who at one time had a shoemaker's shop and business at Doverhay, next to the present Car Park. An old uncle of his, Mr Jim Sparks, who lived at the top of Villes Lane, was sitting on a wall outside his home watching the traffic go by. It was the day of the stag hounds opening meet in August 1910. He counted 63 cars going towards Lynmouth and he counted 61 coming back. He said: 'I don't know whatever 'tis coming to'. What would he say if he could see how many cars pass through towards Lynmouth today? The first car owned in Porlock was a second hand Peugeot and then a 1903 Wolseley, both owned by Mr Pearce the Tanner. Mr Frank Pocock was his chauffeur. He went to Birmingham to await the making of the Wolseley and then drove it back to Porlock. Mr Pearce's grand-daughter, Miss Joan Pearce, told me that she had ridden the Wolesley as a little girl and laughingly said that when it rained they put up their umbrellas.

There was an old lady in Porlock who was always on the lookout for all she could pick up! The boys would play her up. They would drop a handkerchief attached to a long piece of string. When she thought no one was looking she would pick it up and tuck it under her knicker elastic. Of course the boys would watch and wait long enough, and then give the string a tug and the handerkerchief was pulled out. The same old lady was seen coming out of the door to the Rectory garden and as she came out a heap of apples fell out of her knickers.

Tom Webber was a character who earned his living by picking primroses and whortleberries and selling them during the spring and summer. During the winter he chopped sticks and sold bundles for firelighting and did odd jobs especially for the elderly, sympathetic ladies who could afford to pay him. He lived with his sister and a brother and every evening he would be seen in his bedroom window counting the money which he was always talking about. It was a fact that he did have money invested, but he always exaggerated how much he had. He told me that he had money in 'fower' banks. But if he talked of so many thousand he was referring to shillings not pounds.

One of my grandfather's customers was a Mrs Fowler at West Porlock. Mrs Fowler had a large family and had got behind with her payments. One day she offered him a ham which had been cured and was hung in the chimney place. When Mr Fowler returned he said to his wife: 'Wa's thee done with thic there ham?'. Mrs Fowler replied: I've given 'en to Isaac Burgess to pay the bread bill'. 'Well', said Mr Fowler, 'thee tell Isaac Burgess to bring thic there ham back again'.

A popular activity about a century ago was bird batting. Men would go out at night carrying a long net on two poles stretched over a hedge. Another would hold a lantern behind the net, whilst others walked along the other side, beating the hedge with sticks. The roosting birds would fly out towards the light and get caught in the net, to eventually finish up in a pie. Once my grandmother told me of having blackbird pie when she was young girl, but I remember her telling me off because I had brought home a blackbird's egg which I had taken from the nest. How quickly attitudes change.

Porlock school pupils, with headmaster Mr W.R.Hadley (Porlock historian) left. Mr R. Hawker, right. c.1950.

Prior to 1910 there was a small farm next to the present chapel, with fields stretching down to the beach (Higher Bourne Farm). The farmer was Dick Ridler, known to all as Butcher Dick. He was a butcher in a small way for it is said that he only killed half a bullock a week. Butcher's Plantation just below the village was named after its owner Butcher Dick. Not many have a place on a map named after them, but within the last few years a footpath in Porlock has been named 'Vivian's Way', after the Parish Councillor, Vivian Perkins, who fought to keep it open against all opposition.

The story is told of two elderly ladies who lived in Doverhay. They went on a 'bus to Minehead for their first ever visit to the cinema. It was a cowboy film and to them it must have been very realistic, because as they came out, one said to the other; 'Caw, coon't 'ee smell the gun powder'.

A West Luccombe man, shopping in Minehead, went into Hawkins' Chemist shop for some rat poison. The Chemist asked: 'Rodin?', (a brand of rat poison) 'No', said the man, 'I missed the 'bus and walked all the way'.

When Mr Hadley was teaching at Porlock School, one of H.M. Inspectors arrived during a Scripture lesson. They had been reading the story of the Good Samaritan. The Inspector asked if any boy would repeat the story to him. Being keen for a good impression to be made, Mr Hadley asked Donald who attended sunday school regularly and would certainly know the story well. Donald retold the story of how the man fell among thieves on his journey from Jerusalem to Jericho and how both a Priest and a Levite passed him by. Then he said the Samaritan came along and picked him up and sat him on his ass. At this the whole class burst out laughing and there was uproar. I didn't find out what the Inspector said.

Stories and sayings such as these are not confined to the older generation. Only recently I was talking to a young friend, who told me he had sold his saw bench, having advertised it. I asked if he had sold it to someone local. 'No', he said. 'A chap came from Minehead for it'. When he realised what he had said, we both roared with laughter.

15
THE SECOND WORLD WAR

In 1939 when war was imminent, all villagers went to the village hall to be fitted with gas masks. They were carried over the shoulder, and as the masks were in cardboard boxes they were usually put into a canvas cover. School children had to carry them to school every day.

As the village hall was our main building, and was used for civil defence, it was protected by sandbags. Lorry loads of sand were brought from Minehead and tipped into the roadway where gangs of volunteers filled the bags which were placed around the walls of the hall.

In the early evening of September 1st, the first evacuees arrived from West Ham, having been brought to Minehead by train, then on to Porlock by bus. Mrs Rawles, the Postmaster's wife, was in charge of billeting, and after being given tea, the children were sent out with their teachers to various houses in the village, some to live with families, and some in a community at 'Glen Lodge'. Later on mothers with babies also arrived, as well as elderly women. Some more wealthy people came privately and rented accommodation. This influx of people made a great difference. The village children, most of whom had never been to London or even further than Bristol, soon made friends with the West Ham children and quickly picked up London speech and sayings. It wasn't long before the Londoners were imitating our broad dialect, which was much more noticeable in 1939 than at the present time.

War was declared on Sunday, September 3rd, 1939, at 11 am and after the first bombing of Bristol more evacuees arrived. A tea company, Dickson Anderson of Cannon Street, London, had offices in part of 'The Laurels', (now Abbeyfield). The C.H.A. was taken for a children's nursery, as were Holnicote House and Ashley Combe House. The village school was packed to capacity, and the methodist hall and the Victoria Rooms were used for extra classes. Older boys repaired shoes for the children in the TocH room, which was then next to 'Burley' in Parson Street and had been taken over and converted to a meeting place by TocH members in 1937. It was formerly a bakery and then a painter's store.

A collection of waste paper and metal was started: volunteers stored and sorted paper in a stable belonging to Mrs Cape. Old iron was dumped at the Tannery. A special request was made for aluminium and householders gave whatever aluminium saucepans they could spare. They were collected at the shop opposite the Royal Oak, which soon became full.

All buildings were blacked out and this caused considerable work, especially as large buildings and shop windows had to have either dark curtains or shutters which could be put up as darkness came. The few street lights had shields over them; cars and even bicycles had to use shielded lights and pedestrians used torches with paper over the glass with only a small hole for the light. Some windows high up in the church and chapel were permanently blacked out with thick brown paper.

Air raid wardens were appointed and special police enrolled, some full time. The Observer Corps was formed and several men manned the observation post in Sparkhayes Lane in shifts, day and night, between their normal jobs. All aircraft movements were recorded, the post having a direct telephone communication with the Observer Corps at Yeovil. Other Observer posts were at Exford and Dunster.

A force of the Local Defence Volunteers was set up, and the men not in the army, began to train during evenings and on Sunday mornings. All members wore an arm-band with the initials L.D.V. (the local lads quickly referred to them as the 'Look, Duck and Vanish' brigade). Some members took their shotguns along, as no rifles were yet available. Eventually equipment began to arrive as well as uniforms. The officers were mainly elderly retired officers from the first world war. The L.D.V. became the Home Guard and they manned a look-out on Porlock Hill. When not on duty they slept in a hut at Pitt Coombe Head. Invasion was expected at any time but the men had very little means of defence. One man owned a motor-bike, so he was their despatch rider. Porlock platoon was also lucky in that one of its

Home Guard. Porlock Weir, 1945.

Home Guard. Porlock, 1945.

members, Henry Webb, owned a large fast 4 litre Lagonda car. Porlock could boast of being a fast mobile unit, that could travel up the straight past 'Holmbush' to Whitstones at 80 mph. Although training continued throughout the war, the Home Guard, fortunately, were never needed for action but tragically, one of the Selworthy members, Mr Farmer, was accidentally shot and killed, whilst a sten gun was being demonstrated. Their ammunition dump was in the Commanding Officer's garden in Doverhay, the stores were at Holnicote Stables and later at the building where

Miles' Tea offices now are. The firing range for practice was in 'Granny's Ride'.

As part of the defence of the coast, numerous pill boxes were built and miles of barbed wire coils were stretched along the top of the beach. Pill boxes were also placed at strategic points commanding roads. Poles about 7 feet high covered some of the larger fields and piles of stones were heaped on the marsh. This was to discourage or wreck any aircraft or gliders if they attempted to land.

To keep watch on the shipping activities there were the

Coast Guards who manned the look-out at Hurlstone Point continuously. Two special coast guards patrolled the beach to look for anything washed ashore or unexploded mines. Mr Jack Marley patrolled each day from Hurlestone to Porlock Weir and Mr Ewart Perkins from Porlock Weir to Embelle Wood Beach.

The army moved into Porlock in 1940 after the Dunkirk evacuation. The 58th company of Royal Engineers drove down from Barton Stacey and were billeted in the Tannery. Officers and N.C.Os had billets at 'Frazers' and the 'Cottage' guesthouse. They specialised in chemical warfare. It was thought that perhaps the Germans would use gas, as they did in the 1914-18 war. The R.E.s trained on Exmoor and experimented with the firing of gas shells from the rocket-launchers mounted on the backs of lorries. On one occasion a couple of live shells were fired by accident. The Royal Engineers stayed for over a year until they were sent to India. Several married local girls and returned to live in Porlock after the war.

ENSA concert parties came to entertain the troops and civilians at the village hall. The troops also put on their own concerts and dances, providing their own bands. Special days were set aside for fund-raising for war weapons, perhaps to help buy a warship or a 'Spitfire' fighter. Children helped by organising concerts and adults arranged other special events.

Occasional training manoeuvres were held on Exmoor and sometimes the Methodist hall would be used for soldiers to sleep. There was almost a continuous flow of people and traffic through the village. Miles of field telephone cable were laid temporarily along the roads during these operations. Much of Exmoor was a firing range for guns and mortars. A tank firing range was set up on North Hill which had been used occasionally as a training ground from 1890. Civilians were totally excluded from many of these areas. In some places a red flag was flown during firing times. From Porlock one could see one of the dummy tanks on rails which ran along parts of Selworthy Hill and were used as targets.

We must not forget the ladies' part in the war effort. Volunteers ran a canteen for the troops at Greenaleigh Dairy, others were members of the V.A.D. Red Cross and trained in nursing and first aid. The Porlock detachment was formed during the First World War, when several members worked at Minehead Hospital nursing wounded soldiers sent back from the front. Land Army girls were billeted in the village and worked with the men on forestry works and on farms. Girls also took over the local roundsmen's jobs for the first time.

Fire fighting and first aid lectures were held regularly, attended by Red Cross, A.R.P. and Boy Scouts. An Air Training Corps for boys met in the Old Mill in Hawkcombe. The Army Cadets and the Red Cross shared a hut at High Bank, near Splat Barn.

Those of us who were children at the time have many memories. I think we all felt confident of final victory and didn't worry, perhaps, as much as adults. We were always interested in the military activities and took for granted the guards with fixed bayonets posted at the entrance to the Tanyard and the army lorries kept under guard in the rick yard at Court Place Farm and at Glen Lodge stables in Hawkcombe. The vehicles were maintained by army personnel and civilian mechanics at the Central Garage. At Pollard's West End Garage, the workshops were converted to making parts for outboard engines for motor boats for military use.

Most private cars were laid up. Only people with essential needs such as doctors, farmers and traders were allowed petrol. Civilians seldom went beyond Minehead. If a vehicle had to be left unattended, especially at night, the rotor arm would be removed, important in case of invasion. This all seems incredible now but everything was taken very seriously, as we saw other countries in Europe gradually succumb to Hitler and the Nazis.

As the war progressed the USA came into it and it wasn't long before we had American GIs stationed at the Tannery replacing the Royal Engineers. They drove everywhere in their small jeeps and 4-wheel drive vehicles. They also used small 'Piper Cub' aeroplanes and landed in Long Back, the largest field on Court Place Farm. The American army had a very accurate gun on Bossington Hill which fired at a target in the sea off 'Glenthorne'. One Sunday morning, during service time, the whine of a shell was heard as it passed over the village. It fell in a field just in front of the first cottages in West Porlock much to the consternation of the army, who came tearing down in their jeeps. Fortunately there was no damage to life or property.

At Stenthill, near Yearnor Farm, the R.A.F. had a small detachment who never talked about their work. After the war we heard that they had been in communication with Cardiff and first heard about radar for detecting enemy planes. We suspected that this had been the work of this unit. Later a Radar Station was built near East Myne.

The noise of aircraft training was heard every day, especially in good weather. Although Porlock escaped the bombs, the bombing of Swansea could be clearly seen at night. There was a search light battery of troops stationed near Culbone Stables and another at Webber's Post. A few bombs dropped beside the Dunkery road and near Nutscale, leaving huge craters. I remember one night a plane flew very low over the roofs and I jumped out of bed and lay on the floor. The next morning we heard that the soldiers at Webber's Post had fired on it with their rifles.

Several aircraft came down in the valley and there was great excitement when, despite the tall posts, a Wellington bomber made a forced landing in Long Back on February 22nd, 1942. When the plane was repaired they knocked down three hedges ready for take-off. A test pilot came from Filton to fly it. The plane started from near the Weir road by the pound and taxied down across the fields, but stopped again near the bottom by Coy Barn. That was the trial run! The plane taxied back and turned for a new attempt, with nearly half the village looking on. Several men and boys were asked to hang on to the tail plane. Then the pilot revved up the engines to power, the men let go, and the plane taxied fast down over the fields again. Suddenly up came the tail, and the plane lifted off, skimming over the reed bed and just clear of the beach before banking to turn up Channel and make its way back to Weybridge.

During the afternoon of July 26th, 1941, while there were children playing in the recreation ground, a Spitfire flew over low and lowered its wheels. It flew back and forth about three times. No one realised that the pilot wanted to land.

Finally, it flew down towards the sea and made a forced landing in a cornfield. Two boys ran up and the pilot asked them where the Post Office was so that he could phone. They directed him up Pound Lane to the village. Crashed aircraft were often being transported back through the village on 60ft long articulators.

One very bad crash occurred at Ashley Combe: on the foggy morning of June 11th 1943 a British Halifax 4-engined bomber came in from the sea, crashed into the woods and caught fire. The men working in the woods and at the saw mill in Worthy Combe, ran to help. Three men, H. Pollard, T. Cook and J. Ridler tried to get the airmen out, but there was an explosion and Jack Ridler of Porlock Weir was very severely burned. He had to spend some time in hospital. At that time Ashley Combe House was used as a childrens' nursery by Dr Barnados. The plane had just skimmed past the windows at the back of the house, literally within inches. Had the plane hit the house there would have been an even bigger tragedy. As it was, four of the crew were killed and two injured. A memorial was later put up in the wood.

Often out to sea, convoys of ships were seen bringing supplies from America. One morning I went over to the butcher's shop near the school and happened to look out to sea. I saw a large ship going down Channel. Suddenly, and very quickly, her bows went up into the air and she sank stern first. It all happened in a few moments, probably the result of a mine or perhaps a U-Boat. U-Boats operated in the Channel and parachute mines were dropped by German aircraft – two Minehead boatmen were killed by one of these mines. The beach became thick with huge lumps of oil which were left to disperse naturally.

At the beginning of the war the government introduced rationing of foodstuffs, and although prices rose, everyone was allowed their ration, unlike the First War when the poor suffered badly. There was a scheme devised by Williton RDC for the making of meat pies. These were made by Burgess's at Porlock and sold by the Women's Institute.

Prior to D-Day the build up of troops and aircraft increased. Training was stepped up and we saw many gliders being towed by aeroplanes, as well as large pontoons for the

Mulberry Harbour being towed down Channel by tugs.

Because of censorship during the war, very little military activity was reported in the local paper, only the usual items and adverts of interest to the general public. The national daily papers and radio did give a good idea of the progress and setbacks of the war effort, and as many people attended cinemas, the 'newsreel' kept us up to date.

Being a country area and free from bombing, most people fared well in Porlock, although, sad to say, many families lost loved ones as a result of the war. The memorial to the fallen of the First War was erected in 1921. A cross of Doulton stone recorded 24 Porlock men killed. After the Second War the plaque was recarved and the lettering made smaller so that 13 more names could be added.

16
THE JUNKERS
AND THE LIBERATOR

A German Junkers 88 was shot down on to Porlock Beach during the Battle of Britain on September 27th, 1940.

At the time I was a boy attending school in Minehead but on that Friday morning I was at home in Porlock, having felt unwell. Suddenly I heard planes overhead and people shouting in the street. I jumped out of bed and looking out of the window saw a Spitfire doing the victory roll and heard people shout that a German plane was down. Immediately all thought of sickness left me! I pulled on my clothes, left the house and ran through the street with all the others. When I got to the pound at the top of High Bank I joined Miss Doris Ridler of Doverhay Farm who arrived at the same time on her bike. Together we ran across Court Place fields, through Long Back to the marshes and on to New Works. We arrived just in time to see three German prisoners come over the top of the beach with several men escorting them.

I well remember how they were dressed. They were wearing forage caps and one was very tall. I remember old Farmer Dave Ridler saying: 'They've got 'em'. It was said later that he was waving a pitch fork, but as this was quite a common farm implement to be carrying in those days it didn't register with me.

Most of the men were workmen who had been building the pill boxes all along the beach. I believe only one Englishmam was armed and that was a naval officer who always wore a pistol in a holster. He was in charge of a salvage party who had been working on a Fleet Air Arm plane; a 'Fairy Albacore', which had, a fortnight before, made a forced landing on the marsh at Sparkhayes.

The German prisoners walked quietly across the marsh and were driven away in Mr Jim Pollard's car together with P.C. Curtis and escorted by Mr Bert Rice on his pony. They were taken to Minehead Police Station. The rear gunner, Corporal Wilhelm Reuhl, had been killed. His body was brought out later and, covered with a blanket, lay on the top of the beach. He was buried in Porlock Cemetery. The prisoners were interred in a P.O.W. camp in Canada for the rest of the war.

I, and many others, went to the top of the beach where we could see the plane lying at low water mark near Redsands. It was a JU 88, a fighter bomber capable of speeds exceeding 300 mph. It carried a crew of four and was armed with three machine guns, hand held. No one approached the plane because we were told there were unexploded bombs aboard. An army guard was soon on the scene and, of course, the tide soon covered the plane. On Saturday sightseers came from miles around and took away parts of the plane for souvenirs. The machine guns were given to Minehead School Air Training Corps.

Mr Andy Hyde, now of Brandish Street, was a sergeant in the School Air Training Corps and he was responsible for

The Junkers 88 bomber on Porlock Beach. September 1940.

cleaning and renovating the machine guns of the plane. He told me the guns were Rheinmetal Borsig. The boys not only had the guns, but also some ammunition and like true schoolboys, he and his pals fired a gun from his bedroom window. There are still marks of the tracer bullets on the chimney of the house in Minehead.

The plane which had been carrying highly sophisticated photographic equipment in order to photograph the dock gates of the Manchester Ship Canal had been chased from the Bristol area by three Spitfires shooting as it flew over Minehead. My friends at school had also had an exciting time! Ignoring their Air Raid Drill, they all rushed out onto the verandahs and the masters had to shout at them to come back.

The plane then flew very low down the Porlock Vale, smoke pouring from one engine. Mr Ernie Pollard of Porlock Weir who was feeding his chickens when he saw the planes approaching said the Junkers flew over the beach out to sea and then turned shorewards and made a perfect landing in shallow water. Two of the Spitfires had returned and the final credit went to Pilot Officer Eric Mars of 152 Squadron. He later lost his life, shot down over Brest in 1941.

After a few days the plane was washed up by the high tides to the top of the beach, I well remember this, as whilst playing on the plane I slid off the slippery wing and fell into the sea and had to walk home completely soaked.

Those were days when people were dedicated to total war, and yet the prisoners were treated kindly and respect was given to the dead man's grave.

The pilot, Helmut Ackenhauser, the tall man I had noticed, has since returned and visited Minehead Police Station, where he had his photograph taken in the cell he occupied in 1940. He also met Mr. Eddie Jones who has tended the grave of the rear gunner. The family of Wilhelm Reuhl who was barely 18 years old when he was killed, have also visited the grave, one of the best kept in the cemetery. Later I met Wilhelm Reuhl's brother whilst he was on a visit from Germany. He was eight years old when his brother was killed.

Many people ask about the Monument on Porlock marsh. This is to the memory of the United States airmen whose plane crashed in the marsh on October 29th, 1942. Our American allies were then operating in England. The plane was a long range Bomber, Transport and Reconnaissance Aircraft, its full title being Consolidated B-24 D. Liberator. The plane had four 1200 h.p. Radial engines; a wing span of 110 feet, and a total of length 67 feet 2 inches. Maximum speed 300 m.p.h. at 30,000 feet; range 2100 miles. It carried a crew of 12 and had 10 .50 machine guns.

This particular plane which was helping R.A.F. Coastal Command at that time, took off from Holmsley, South Hampshire, at 7.20am on October 29th, to fly on anti-submarine patrol in the Bay of Biscay. When it was returning at about 3.30pm it was seen by two boys, Alan Perkins and Brian Richards, to hit the top of Bossington Hill and swing round. Pieces fell off, a wheel and part of the undercarriage were lying at the bottom of Sparkhayes Lane and the rest of the plane crashed onto the marsh. The weather was dreadful, a very wet day with low cloud all around. Amongst the first on the scene was Mr Cecil Westcott, Nurse Bragg, the

The Liberator Monument on Porlock Marsh.

District Nurse, and members of the Observer Corps. Mr Westcott carried the nurse through the swamp to the plane, but little could be done. Only one man, S/Sgt. H.B. Thorpe was still alive. Very little of the plane was seen by local people, as its remains were salvaged within a few days.

The simple monument was erected by members of the Porlock Branch of the British Legion, with materials available at that time. The monument has, as most will know, been moved from its original site and now more people are able to see it. The crew are buried at the Americal Military Cemetery in Cambridge. The one unknown on the Memorial was Sgt. S.C. Prekel.

17
THE LAST
TWO HUNDRED YEARS

Picture in your mind the Porlock of 1779 when the Poet Laureate, Robert Southey stayed at the Ship Inn on August 9th. During his stay he described Porlock as being a place known as the end of the world by some folk, because there was no road for wheeled vehicles beyond. The hill farms were still using sleds to move hay for fodder and bedding for the animals. The rain kept him inside by the ale-house fire, a spot still known as 'Southey's Corner'. Whilst he was confined indoors he wrote the Sonnet to Porlock which was published in the 'Morning Post', on August 26th.

Porlock, thy verdant vale so fair to sight,
Thy lofty hills which fern and furze embrown.
The waters that roll musically down
Thy wooded glens, the traveller with delight
Recalls to memory, and the Channel grey
Circling its surges in thy level bay.
Porlock, I also shall forget thee not
Here by the unwelcome summer rain confined
But often shall hereafter call in mind
How here, a patient prisoner, 'twas my lot
To view the lonely, lingering close of day
Making my sonnet by the ale-house fire
Whilst idleness and solitude inspire
Dull rhymes to pass the duller hours away.

The poet Coleridge, a contemporary of Southey and Wordsworth lived for a time at Nether Stowey. During this time he walked with his friends on the Quantocks and Exmoor. It was while he was staying, in the summer of 1787, at a lonely farm – believed to be Ash Farm – between Porlock and Lynmouth, that he began his poem 'Kubla Khan'. A visitor, a man from Porlock, called and by so doing broke his train of thought. The lines were lost forever, and the poem was never finished. The man from Porlock, however, is reprimanded for all time by lovers of poetry.

By 1840-60 the population of Porlock was a little larger. Most people worked on the land and lived in cob and thatch cottages. There were a few shopkeepers. The 1851 census gives the population of the whole Parish as 854; Porlock Town, 448; Bossington, 128.

The census of 1851 was the first to ask for the birthplace. Of the 176 heads of families and their wives in Porlock and Bossington, 47% were born outside Porlock. Only 9 people were over 70, the oldest being a man of 82. There were 111 children in Porlock Town, of whom 76 were listed as scholars. Their age range was from 4 to 13.

Porlock by 1869 was still fairly self-supporting; a small sea port at Porlock Weir and a market town ruled by the Vestry who still appointed two overseers of the poor and two waywardens each year. It was mainly an agricultural area but the village produced most goods that were needed: footwear,

The Ship Inn, Porlock, c.1900-10.

Occupations - Porlock Town:

Occupation	Count	Occupation	Count
Farming	33	Tailors	7
Labourers	27	Dressmakers	7
House Servants	13	Drapers	3
Charwomen	2	Seamstress	1
Artist	1	Straw Bonnet-Maker	1
Masons	15	Shop-Keepers	3
Carpenters	6	Innkeepers	5
Thatchers	2	Millers	2
Painters	1	Bakers	3
Mariners	2	Cheese-Dealers	2
Tanners	2	Tallow-Chandlers	2
Bootmakers	4	Carrier	1
Cordwainers	9	Teachers	3
Relieving Officer	1	Doctor	1
Blacksmiths	5	Letter Carriers	1
Coopers	4	Sawyers	2
Groom	1	Out of Service	4
Rector	1		

clothing, carts and tools. It also had the Tannery. Village life revolved more around the church. The then Rector, the Rev. Sylvanus Brown, is reputed to have refereed boxing matches on the bridge. Boxing replaced the former vicious sport of wrestling, which allowed the contestants to wear iron-shod boots in order to kick their opponents' shins the harder and knock them off balance. The old chapel which had opened in 1837 was also very active.

Communications were improving. The first stage-coach came in 1843 and a carrier called at the village every Friday. The Penny Post had started in 1840 and letters arrived at 8.55am and were collected at 5.30pm.

There were the Old and New Clubs, forerunners of the Friendly Societies. The Old Club dated back to 1776 and the New Club to 1819. They were organised for mutual support in time of sickness and distress and also helped with the cost of funerals. The Club Day with processions and feasting often lasted three or four days! The Minehead and Dunster Village Hospital was opened in Dunster in 1867 and there were also the village charities. In 1876 a branch of the Ancient Order of Foresters was formed and for a while was very active. There are still a few members.

There was no compulsory education but a small school was open in Parson Street, the schoolmaster receiving a salary of £32 a year. There was a dame-school at Porlock Weir. The new school was opened for all in 1876.

Wages were between six and seven shillings a week but the cost of food was comparable: for example, a pound of sugar, 3d., a pound of cheese 9d., a pound of tea, 2s.6d. a cwt of coal, $8\frac{1}{2}$d. beefsteak, $7\frac{1}{4}$d. a pound, chops $2\frac{3}{4}$d. a pound, the main diet of the villagers was fish and potatoes. The oyster beds were fished from 1870 and although most were sent to Bristol, many were eaten locally as the shells found in village gardens testify. Beer was popular since tea was so expensive.

Cricket was played in 1865 and the cricket field was first mentioned in 1877. It was on glebe land and later became the Recreation Ground. Rugby football was being played in 1882 but in 1887 soccer started. The transition to the new game must have been difficult as the press reported that in one of the early football matches 'one of the Porlock team picked up the ball and ran'.

Horse bus on the bridge c.1912.

In 1891 the church was extensively restored and in the same year the new cemetery was opened in Hawkcombe on land actually belonging to Luccombe Parish, which was unfortunate for Porlock folk, because they had to pay for burial, whereas Luccombe parishoners were buried free!

The village began to be known as a centre for hunting and tourists. By 1894 there were coaches to Minehead three times a week in winter and daily in summer months. Also in that year a lending library of 300 volumes was opened. The library continued in Dovery Manor which had been re-stored by Sir Charles Chadwyck-Healey and was run by volunteers up to 1969. The building also housed the Reading Room from 1899 and still continues as a Billiard and Snooker Club with a Museum and Information Centre.

Building changes reflected the influx of visitors. In 1886 the Three Horse Shoes Inn was closed and sold for £600 and a new hotel known as the Lorna Doone Hotel was built on the site. The old Castle Inn was sold in 1887 for £900, and rebuilt as the Castle Hotel in 1890. In 1893 up to a dozen cottages which surrounded the churchyard were demol-

Porlock Band, 1875.

ished in order to widen Parson Street and in 1897, at the time of Queen Victoria's Diamond Jubilee, the Victoria Rooms were opened, the top room used for church meetings and the bottom room as a Reading Room for the village men. This at a cost of £250.

Porlock would have been very different, perhaps, had the proposed railway in 1885 from Porlock Weir to Minehead and the 1898 proposed railway from Minehad to Lynmouth materialised. This project was on the cards for a number of years, as was Mr Knight's proposed railway bringing iron ore from Simonsbath to Porlock Weir, another enterprise which failed.

So we come to 1900, when the first motor car climbed Porlock Hill, thus starting a new era for Porlock. Wages had risen to 10s. per week, 9s. for a farm labourer. It was still a long day's work at the Tannery, with a half day on Saturday

Porlock Band, 1953. Coronation celebrations. Disbanded late '50s.

starting at 4p m. Electricity came in 1911. The Porlock Electric Company was formed and electricity was produced by the water mill in Hawkcombe.

In August 1910 the new Golf Links on Porlock Marsh were formally opened by the Countess of Lovelace, President of the Club. The links were provided by an enterprising company of enthusiasts calling themselves the Porlock Golf Company and many people took up shares at 5s. each.

The 9 hole course had been laid out by Messrs Huish and Cooksley, builders, on Mr Blathwayt's land under the direction of Mr Benge, a golf professional. Bunkers and access bridges, some still there, were built with the only access down Sparkhayes Lane. At the bottom there was a raised path through the fields, should the lane be too muddy. It was hoped to improve the lane later so that motor cars could go right to the bottom thus avoiding a long walk for the members before they started to play.

Opening of Golf Course, 1910.

Receipt for shares.

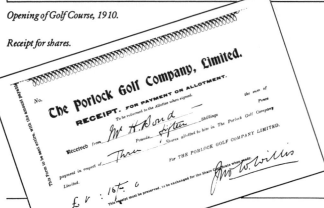

The course was described as being in the 'most charming place' by Sir Francis Gould in his remarks proposing a vote of thanks to Lady Lovelace. He said that it did not take very long, even to a casual visitor to Porlock, to get attached to that beautiful place.

Two foursome parties played the first game on the 9 hole course and afterwards tea was provided by Mrs S. Stenner of Porlock. The club house, where the players could leave their clubs under the care of the professional Mr Benge, is now a ruin. There was also a club house in the village sited opposite the Castle Hotel which was used for social events.

Golf Club site.

It was planned to increase the course to 18 holes but unfortunately, that autumn, the high tides washed away most of the course dashing any further hopes of using it as a tourist attraction.

Porlock has always been a sociable place with its clubs and societies. As far back as 1903 the Porlock Choral Society had a fine choir, performing works like 'Merry Old England' (1903), 'The King of Sherwood' (1908), 'Ali Baba and the Forty Black Sheep' (1909), 'The Mandarin' (1910), 'The Dogs of Devon' (1935) and in 1936 'Hiawatha' as well as a performance of Handel's 'Messiah'. The first concerts were held in the school but in 1925 the village hall was opened. The Parson Street Reading Room put on a popular concert each year.

Since then many village events have been held: whist drives, dances, and the annual horticultural shows. There were local shows: the 'Smugglers' and a sequel to 'Lorna Doone', with music and lyrics by local young people and produced by the Guides and Scouts. In recent years local productions of pantomimes have proved popular. In winter months, parties for children and older folk, organised by the British Legion, TocH and the Women's Institute were eagerly looked forward to. Another annual event enjoyed by old and young alike was the visit of the circus: Sangers, Robert Fossett and Bertram Mills, who brought their horses, lions and elephants.

Carnivals have resumed in recent years, starting with the 1969 'Lorna Doone' centenary events. It was whilst watching this carnival that someone was heard to remark how good it was for Porlock's first carnival. An 80 year old standing near me said: 'I can remember carnivals when I was a boy in Porlock'. Nothing is new!

From 1900 onward things improved in the village although life changed quite slowly. Except for the people who had moved here and built homes, the working people and farmers and shop-keepers were in the main from families who had lived in the area for generations. The motor car was seen occasionally, particularly in summer time. Shops were growing in number, roads improving, although the main street wasn't tarred until after the First World War. The dust in summer time was kept down by Mr Ridler of Doverhay Farm with a water cart, at the cost of 3s. per day. Because Mr Ridler was paid by Porlock Parish Council, he didn't water the side of the Main Street which was in Luccombe Parish (ie Doverhay).

At the beginning of the century there was a horse bus service to Minehead, but in the 1920s the 'Blue Motor' Company started a sterling service which ran to the late '50s. In the 1930s the Mascot Company ran a service which was taken over by the Western National and today we have Southern National and Scarlet Coaches.

If anyone was ill the hospital was now at Minehead and there was also a large Isolation Hospital built at Venniford (now private dwellings). Isolation cases were first admitted into a temporary hospital at Tivington.

Most of the men worked in the village and some children attended the new secondary school at Minehead after 1929. The place of assembly in the village was the bridge where a crowd of men would gather during the dinner hour. They would wait until a few minutes before 2pm, before dispersing to the various places of employment. Early in the century when young women went out to service they often married the local village men. Everything carried on peacefully except, of course, for the interruption of two world wars. It was due to these events that there was more movement of population and men afterwards brought home wives from places far away from Porlock.

The Boy Scouts, formed in Porlock as early as 1909 by Mr Salaman the owner of Doverhay Place, could boast a drum and bugle band in those days. Scouts have continued, although with a few breaks, until today. Guiding was started in Porlock after the First War by Miss Holmes, the Rector's daughter, and was later followed by Cubs and Brownies, all of which have had their ups and downs, as have the Youth Clubs.

Even with the coming of cars, horse riding for pleasure has always been popular and there were always hacks and hunters for hire. Mr Joe Collins came in the 1920s from Exeter, the founder of the Porlock Vale Riding School. He was succeeded by his son Tony, well known in the equestrian world. He trained the British Olympic Team at Porlock in 1952 for the Olympic Games in Helsinki. Unfortunately he lost his life in an aeroplane crash in the Mediterranean. Polo was also popular and games were played in a field at Newbridge.

After the Second World War the tourist boom was on and great trade was done by some villagers in Bed and Breakfast. Nearly everyone arrived by train to Minehead and on by bus to Porlock. As the motor car began to appear again after the war, the private Bed and Breakfast trade declined, the trend in holidays changing and visitors more likely to go into hotels and guest houses. Camping was also becoming more popular as better equipment became available.

Before the war large camps of Scouts, Guides and other groups were dotted around all the farms during the summer, but they are now confined mainly to the camp site at Horner.

Early in the century families would go off to pick 'worts' (whortleberries) during the summer school holidays, a real source of income for poorer people, who often used the extra money to buy clothes. In 1938 worts were sold to the dealers for 4d. per quart (they were always measured in a

THE PORLOCK TROOP BOYSCOUTS. LE VOWLES POR.

Scouts 1910.

Guides outing to Woody Bay, c.1920.

quart measure) after the leaves had been fanned out with a tea tray as the worts were dropped onto a sheet. When the war came the price rose to 2s. – 2s.6d. a quart. Mr Cecil Westcott, the Porlock fruiterer, used to buy worts and collect them from pickers on Exmoor. The fruit was then taken to Minehead Station and sent to London and the cities in the Midlands, mostly for human consumption although a blue dye could be made from them. The largest amount sent by Mr Westcott by train, was the incredible amount of one ton all packed in small punnets. After the war, with higher wages, wort picking declined and many of the favourite hills were converted to pasture. Most people now picking the fruit are visitors who stop their cars and take some home to make whortleberry tart to eat with clotted cream. Even the cream is now unobtainable at the farms!

Social changes have brought greater mobility of labour, consequently fewer people spend their entire life in one place. Many people now retire here.

In previous days people's lives were centred around one community: life and death were celebrated by the whole community, because everyone knew each other.

I am thankful that I grew up in Porlock from the time of it being a small close knit community with practically free access to a much more uncultivated and less intensively farmed Exmoor.

I hope that all may enjoy Porlock and its surroundings and that we may be able to keep it unspoiled, although we may have to accept many changes. Residents of Porlock today can be thankful for the changes and its way of life, and its beautiful surroundings. I myself love it and have no wish to live anywhere else.

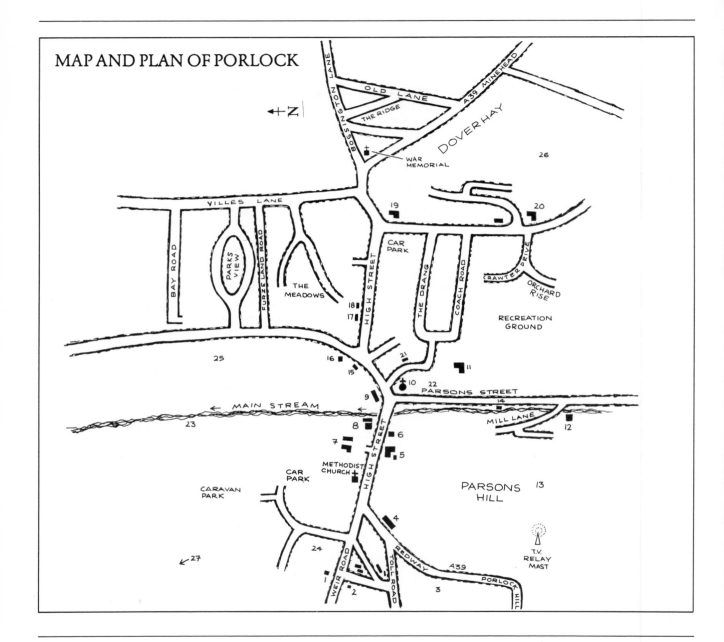

MAP AND PLAN OF PORLOCK

MAP AND PLAN OF PORLOCK

1. The Pound. Splat Barn

2. Court Place.

3. The Parks and Conygar.

4. Ship Inn.

5. Castle Inn.

6. Town Mill.

7. The Tannery.

8. Market Place

9. Rose and Crown

10. Church.

11. The Rectory.

12. Hawkcombe Mill.

13. Parsons Hill.

14. The Old School.

15. Chapel.

16. Sparkhayes.

17. Three Horse Shoes.

18. Royal Oak.

19. Doverhay Manor.

20. Doverhay Farms.

21. The Priests' House.

22. Houses Round the Church.

23. Mesne Stream.

24. The Buttyard.

25. The Field.

26. Doverhay – Luccombe.

27. The Decoy – Coy Barn.

1. The Pound
For impounding stray animals, used within living memory. The present pound has been built since 1844. Previously the pound was on the left of the old entrance to Court Place.

Splat Barn
Splat means allotment, so possibly some connection with the Manor Strip system. The house is marked as a building of historic interest on the 6 inch map of 1929.

2. Court Place
Court Place is where the Lord of the Manor lived. In 1420 the Manor House had a hall and a Great Chamber. In 1640, Gerard says 'not farre from the Town you may see an Ancient Manor House'. The house was burnt down in the early nineteenth century and a new house built on a site nearby. The Manor Court was still being held in 1842.

3. The Parks and Conygar
The Parks were useful for keeping pigs. Tenants paid 2d. for woodweyght and 1d. for ferneheu. The first was the right to take wood and the second the right to take fern.

The Coney-garth or Coney-acre was where the Lord of the Manor caught his rabbits.

The old Castle Inn. Porlock Weir horse bus on right.

The new Castle Hotel. c.1900.

4. Ship Inn

In 1797 the Poet Laureate, Robert Southey, stayed at the Ship Inn and while there wrote the poem beginning 'Porlock, thy verdant vale'.

5. The Castle Inn

Once thatched, the old Castle Inn was sold in 1887 for £900, then demolished to make way for the present Castle Hotel.

6. Town Mill

Now the Mill Wheel Gallery, once the Manor or Town Mill. The 20 customary tenants of 1306 were bound by agreement to clean out the mill pond on Hockday (second Tuesday after Easter). In the bailiff's rolls of 1419-26 Lady Harrington had to spend much money to keep the mill in repair.

7. The Tannery

Once Porlock's largest industry. Here leather was produced. The Tanyard is first mentioned in 1794 belonging to Abraham Phelps. It closed after the First World War.

8. Market Place

A weekly market and two or three annual fairs granted in 1366 and again in 1614. Tradition speaks of a 'beautiful market house,' but where it was is not known. There was still a Market Cross in 1810. On the Tithe Map of 1844 there is a small building near the Central Garage, parallel to the river, which is called the Market House. Markets disappeared c.1800, and fairs c.1870.

9. Rose and Crown Inn

Only two Inns are mentioned in a directory of 1794; the Ship and the Rose and Crown. In 1870 the landlady was summoned for rowdy behaviour in the Inn. It was closed down about 1880. It is believed that R.D. Blackmore stayed at the Rose and Crown.

10. The Church of St Dubricius

The earliest part of the church dates from the thirteenth century. Probably rebuilt by Sir Simon Fitzroges about 1300. His effigy is in the church. St Dubricius was a Welsh saint and it seems very likely that West Somerset was Christianised from Wales. Probably the church was built on the same site as used for pagan worship.

Court Place Farm. Site of original manor. Manor Court held here.

The Royal Oak and Three Horse Shoes.

Dovery Manor. Formerly Dovery Court, built c. 1450.

Copy of painting by A. Carruthers Gould. Looking up to Parsons Hill. Note entrance to churchyard through archway, and old chapel on the right.

11. The Rectory
Part of the Rectory goes back to the fifteenth century or earlier. The first Porlock Rector was John, son of Rogo, appointed in 1297. From 1559 the living has been in the gift of the Crown.

12. Hawkcombe Mill
or Parsonage Mill. This was the Rector's mill as it was in the Rectorial Manor.

13. Parsons Hill
So called because it belonged to the Church Manor. Also called Burley Hill.

14. The Old School
Before the present school opened in 1876 there was a schoolroom in Parson Street, run by subscription. There is mention of a school in 1783 when 11d. tax was paid for School House. In the Tithe Roll there is mention of another schoolroom behind the National Westminster Bank. This in addition to the Parson Street school. Before 1876 there was a dame school at the Weir.

15. The Chapel
The old chapel was built in 1837, now a cafe. The first Methodist services were held in Porlock in 1810. The new chapel opened in 1927.

16. Sparkhayes
Once a farm, Sparkhayes was not a Manor. It was first mentioned in 1383. Once belonged to the Earl of Lovelace.

17. The Three Horse Shoes
This was on the site of the Lorna Doone Hotel. Mentioned in the 1822 Register of Inns, it is also in the 1902 directory. It was knocked down soon afterwards.

18. The Royal Oak
On the Tithe Map there is an inn next door to the Three Horse Shoes called the 'Somerset Inn', owned by Abraham Sparks junior. Probably the Royal Oak.

19. Doverhay Court or Manor
Now the Information Centre, Museum and Snooker Club. It was restored in 1894, 'An example of a remarkably small Manor house of the fifteenth century'. Probably used as a Dower House for the Lady when her husband died. The restoration was paid for by Sir Charles E.H. Chadwyck-Healey. Now owned by Porlock Parish Council.

20. Doverhay Farms and Inns
Both Lower and Higher Doverhay Farms were once the homes of substantial yeomen. They are no longer farms.

There were two taverns in Doverhay in 1280. A man was murdered in one of them, and the whole hundred of Carhampton was fined for the murder.

21. The Priests' House – The Harrington Chantry
The Harrington Memorial in the church is one of the finest of its kind – erected in memory of Lord and Lady Harrington. The first priest was appointed in 1476 and the chantry closed in 1546. The priest had to reside 'in a certain messuage, hard by the cemetery of the church'. The chaplains had to provide bread and cheese and ten gallons of good beer to be eaten and drunk in memory of the Lord and Lady after the anniversary service.

22. Houses Round the Church
These were knocked down about 1890 and the position of the road altered. There was an archway into the church – and here the stocks were kept in the early ninteenth century. A Mr Chibbett, in the latter half of the nineteenth century, rented the room over the archway. One of the houses was a malthouse – of which there were six in Porlock in the early part of the 1800s.

Looking east along the High Street, c1870. The house behind the horse is 'The Laurels' (Porlock Abbeyfield). To the right of the cart is the Castle Inn. The houses facing were at the bottom of Parson Street.

23. Mesne Stream

The Meadowland was held in common, it was the most valued land, and bordered on the stream.

24. The Buttyard

Where archery was practised by order of the king. The field is now covered with bungalows.

25. The Fields

In 1306, 20 villeins held a furlong each, in return for many duties to the Lord of the Manor. The field (ie. the open field) frequently mentioned in the Bailiff's Rolls of 1419-26, but only in connection with haymaking. In 1509 the common fields were called Netherlands, Cowlease, Uppastyle and Pownde Parke. There were also Wheatpark, Buttyard, Allerpark and Conygar.

26. Doverhay – Luccombe

The separation of Doverhay from Porlock goes back at least to Saxon times. The name is possibly British in origin. No reason is known why Luccombe should have this corridor to the Bristol Channel. An attempt was made to join the two parts when the first Parish Council was elected in 1891 – but without success. Doverhay was joined to Porlock civil parish in 1928.

27. The Decoy – Coy Barn

Cygnets were taken from the marsh for the Lady Harrington's table in 1420 – 'the expenses of divers men taking cygnets by order of the Lady; 10d.'

BIBLIOGRAPHY AND SUGGESTED FURTHER READING

Chadwyck-Healey, C. *The History of Part of West Somerset*, Southeran, 1901

Collison-Morley, K. *Porlock, West Porlock, Porlock Weir, and Culbone*, Cox, n.d.

Hurley, J. *Exmoor in Wartime. 1939-45*, Exmoor Press, 1978

Morris, J.(ed) *Domesday Book. (No8) Somerset*, Phillimore, 1980

Page, J.L.W. *An Exploration of Exmoor*, Seeley, 1890

Savage, J. *History of the Hundred of Carhampton*, Strong, 1830

Whyte-Melville, G.J. *Katerfelto. A story of Exmoor*, Chapman and Hall, 1875

Allen, N.V. *Exmoor Place Names*, Alcombe Books, 1986

Pointon, A.G. *Methodism in West Somerset*, P.P., 1982

Bouquet, M. *No Gallant Ship*, Hollis and Carter, 1959

Farr, G. *Somerset Harbours*, Christopher Johnson, 1954

Symons, W. *Early Methodism in West Somerset*, Kelly, 1895

Hook, Rev. Walter M.A. *A History of the Ancient Church of Porlock, and of the Patron Saint, St Dubricius and his Times*, Parker, 1893

Eeles, F.C. *The Church of St Dubricius, Porlock*, Barnicott and Pearce, 1935

Halliday, M. *Description of the Monuments and Effigies in Porlock Church*, Torquay, 1882

Gillman, J. *Nineteenth Century West Somerset Sailing Ships*, Unpublished

Hawkins, M. *Somerset at War 1939-1945*, Dovecote Press, 1988

Marshall, H.J. *Exmoor Sporting and Otherwise*, Eyre and Spottiswoode, 1948

Ridler, J.K. *A Selworthy Notebook*, P.P., 1983

Smith, G. *Smuggling in the Bristol Channel 1700-1850*, Countryside Books, 1989

Waters, B. *The Bristol Channel*, Dent, 1955

View of Porlock, c1910.

ACKNOWLEDGEMENTS

My thanks must go to the many people who, over the years, knowing of my interest in Porlock and its history, have encouraged me to write this book.

To the many local people who have let me talk to them and have given me valuable information of their own memories.

To the Porlock Museum Committee, and especially the late W.R. Hadley who collected so much information which Mrs J. Hadley has kindly allowed me to use.

To my wife who has spent many hours reading over and typing from my longhand writing.

The photographs are mainly from my own colour transparencies and from my collection of old photographs. Some of the old ones are from the Porlock Museum Collection.